Walking
for Creative Recovery

Walking
for Creative Recovery

A handbook for creatives,
with insights and ideas for supporting
your creative life

Christina Reading & Jess Moriarty

Triarchy Press

Published in this first edition in 2022 by:

Triarchy Press
Axminster, UK
www.triarchypress.net

ISBNs:
Print: 978-1-913743-54-3
ePub: 978-1-913743-55-0
PDF: 978-1-913743-56-7

Figures 17 and 22-25 are by Jess Moriarty
Figure 42 is by Tony Gammidge
Both cover illustrations and all other images in this book are by Christina Reading

Acknowledgements

Jess: This book is a collaboration with Chris – it is by her, but it is also because of her and for her. We did not know if we would get there, but kept walking, talking, making, and finally, we did. Let's not stop now. It is also a collaboration with my colleagues and students at the University of Brighton – thank you for walking with me and for being my guides. Especially to Kate Aughterson, Tony Gammidge, Finlay McInally, Barbara Chamberlin, Craig Jordan-Baker, Tony Kalume, Julie Everton, Eleanor Knight, Bea Hitchman, Sarah-Jane Ryan and Mike Hayler – bringers of joy. This book is for my parents who ignited my creativity and for my family who hate walking but who came along with me anyway. Always.

Chris: For Jess, who encouraged me to look forward and to write and my glorious family, my husband John and my children, Lizzie, Katherine and Jimmy, and my beautiful granddaughter Eleanor Rella with love for all the joy you bring.

Contents

Introduction: Our Own Creative Recovery

I expressed some long felt and deeply felt emotion. And in expressing it I explained it and then laid it to rest.

(Woolf: 1989, p.90)

Jess

We got cancer within a year of each other – fuck you, cancer – and for the same and also for different reasons, it left us both feeling lost. Lost because we did not know who these sick women with cancer were and lost because we didn't want to know them. Lost creatively because we felt our creative practice had been stifled – Chris because the paints she used in her artwork are known carcinogens, and me because of my acute realisation that I was addicted to work: to the admin, meetings and committees that all took me away from writing and teaching and left me feeling empty and purposeless. And lost because we didn't know the way back.

When I got skin cancer, my response was to work harder and pretend it wasn't happening. Two days after the melanoma was cut out, I cooked Christmas dinner for 14 people and felt pleased the procedure was done in the holidays, so I didn't need to take a single day off work. Chris was diagnosed with kidney cancer almost a year later and she hunkered down, went off grid, banished friends – me included – from her life while she focused her energies on getting well. Very selfishly, I didn't approve of or want her exile and asked if she would be willing to help me with a book I had committed to and didn't know how to finish. Slightly unwilling at first, she agreed with the caveat that she could back out and return to isolation at any point.

Wanting to resist conventional approaches to academic work (Moriarty: 2014), and because it was an activity we both enjoyed, we chose to walk and talk about our creativity and decided to use this engaged and active process to identify possible solutions to our personal and creative crises. We recorded some of our walks and committed to writing our experiences and seeing what happened. But we just didn't know. We didn't know if Chris would even be well enough or if I could keep focused on this vague approach that didn't have any instant value or the meaning I was used to in academic work. But we both knew we couldn't keep feeling creatively stunted and vowed to at least try. 'Nothing to lose' seemed to drive the project in its early stage. Selfishly, I was motivated by wanting to see my friend working creatively again, certain that it would help her to get over and recover from kidney cancer. In truth, I didn't know if it would. But there are worse motivations than hope.

Figure 1: Hope

Celia Hunt argues that by storying the self, people are able to express themselves in a way that gives them permission to be different (Hunt: 2000) and we both wanted to express ourselves using techniques and methods that were new to us and also to find ways of being that differed from those of patient/person with cancer. Chris suggested places we might walk, and we decided to go somewhere we hadn't explored before and to try and use the feeling of not knowing as a positive challenge. To let go and just see.

"Let's try Chanctonbury Ring?" she offered, a place I hadn't been since I was a child, preferring to walk within a ten-mile radius of my house where I know each step and feel in control of the path I tread.

"It's far enough from home to be new." Chris is very persuasive.

"What if it rains?" I fretted, already panicking, already finding an excuse.

Chris looked me in the eye, "We go no matter what, Jess."

So, we walked, and we wrote, and we didn't use a map, but somehow, we found a way.

> *Reality is unmappable – too big, sprawling and changeable to*
> *be captured entire on paper or canvas. It is like trying to trap*
> *a giant squid with a rock pool net.*
>
> (Macfarlane: 2018, p.33)

Scott-Hoy and Ellis argue that "The art part of the project, which creates moods and images, combines with writing, which is better at directing emotion. In many cases, published words are used more to explain the art, rather than enhance the emotional mood" (2008, p.9) (see also Barone: 2003 and Slattery: 2001). Here we choose not to make the distinction, instead image and text work together to tell an interdisciplinary story about our work as interdisciplinary researchers. Educational researchers, such as Tierney and Lincoln (1997), have suggested that multiple approaches "may represent both the complexity of the lives we study, and the lives we lead as academics and private persons" (p.xi) and we suggest that the mixture of voices, memoir, poetry and painting can offer an insight into this complex time, and the process we used to move past it.

This book offers a "meeting place as a mixed stream of fluids, as something multi-layered, not known, always to be created anew, as the field of many understandings" (Sava & Nuutinen: 2003, p.532) and is connected to notions of intertextuality and the dialogue of texts (Bakhtin, 1981). Our voices intermingle and weave, but also come together to tell our shared story. A story that perhaps explains why this book means so much to us both.

Finding a way back: walking as a method for recovery

Preamble: Chanctonbury Ring to Winston's Vineyard and back

Jess

We are flying as fast as my little red Citroen will allow, through the rain and down roads in West Sussex that move us towards Chanctonbury Ring. The area has a history as an ancient fort used for rituals in the Bronze Age and was once a temple site for Romans.

The local legend is that the devil made the ring of trees and that it can increase the fertility of women who sleep beneath it. That is definitely not the reason either of us is here, but we are looking for change. Chris is recovering from cancer and all the emotional and physical challenges that go with it. Restoring herself has been all consuming and she has been unable to paint through it. Me, I'm writing a book about resisting neoliberalism but I'm so institutionalised that I can't even think about research or writing without clear outputs, impact, strategy. Creativity needs space and freedom but mine feels penned in, stifled; I need to try something new. I need to rewild myself on the South Downs Way.

I've known Chris for about ten years now. We met in a writing workshop for demotivated doctoral students and got chatting, did the 'we should do some work together' thing when we parted and then actually did. Whilst we were interviewing students about their creative processes (Reading & Moriarty: 2010), I fell pregnant with my first child and Chris, with three older children, had great advice and insights on juggling work and motherhood. Her son, Jimmy, jiggled and then chased Reilly for me while we worked in her kitchen and one day, when I felt sick at work, Chris predicted I was pregnant again. When I got home and took a test, it turned out she was right, and that Arla had found a way. I suppose I instinctively looked up to, and still look up to, Chris. It is a shared joke that I covet her huge Brighton home that feels full of love and family history. She says it how she sees it and we have been honest enough with each other over the years that when she says, "you know what I think Jess...", she's usually right. Chris is straight-talking, funny, intelligent and a brilliant artist. We have three of her beautiful paintings in our house. One of a woman in mid-air, and on different days and at different times in my life, I have wondered if she's falling or flying. I think it's okay that I'm never quite sure.

Not just a walk, not just I

Chris

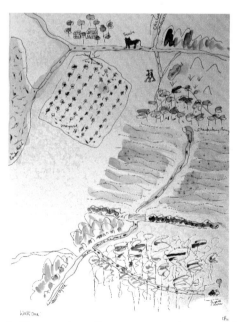

Figure 2: Chanctonbury Ring to Winston's Vineyard and back

This walk feels more formed; it has a purpose, an output, a reason for walking. This walk is no longer simply a means of being and punctuating the space between hospital visits. It will form part of a method for Jess and me to find new creative strategies, to help us forge our way forward – to find a way out of sadness, out of mourning and to do this in a manner that does not deny our illness and losses but seeks to carry them more lightly. These reasons shift the space of walking. It now feels that the walk is part of something other than just me; it is part of a research project. It is linked to another, to my friend and research partner, Jess. We walk – not I – the act is defined by intermingling interaction. It is a collaboration. There is a sense and expectation that the walk needs to offer something, and the expectation of unspoken outputs lingers, whether this will be new writing, new visual work or new personal, academic, creative directions that emerge, is still unknown. No longer just a walk – a walk already framed by intention.

I begin this walk saddened by the loss of health, work and creative direction and feel naked, stripped of all that framed my life, all that I felt certain about, except perhaps walking.

I contemplate why walking took such a central place in my illness and recovery right from the off. After the diagnosis I didn't go home, I went for a walk; it was as if walking somehow helped me to make sense of what I had been told, helped me to traverse the space between the news that I had cancer and my ability to receive and understand what this meant for me. In the lead-up to the operation to remove my tumour, walking gave me a sense that I was helping myself, damping anxiety and fear with physical exhaustion and fresh air. My memory of this time is walking, usually with my husband, John, to places familiar and unfamiliar across Sussex, getting acquainted or reacquainted with its countryside, its towns and villages. There was a rhythm to this time; scary appointments were interspersed with walking, accompanied always by my cancer. I cried before, after and during the walks – walking, crying and cancer soaking the fabric of my new reality.

After the operation, a new pace, a new rhythm, took hold in the days that followed. I marked my progress by how far I could walk – I walked to the toilet, to the end of the corridor. Then, when I got home, I walked upstairs, around the garden, around the kitchen. My horizons extended slowly. I ventured outside and I walked up the street, round the block, round the park, and endlessly along the seafront to a café that I felt I could reach from the car park. Sometimes I over-extended myself and had to go back to bed to recover. Now, in the woods with Jess, I am, and she is, in a new and still unfathomable space. Looking ahead to years of endless monitoring, uncertainty, wondering if every cough or headache or blemish is a step back or a full stop. What punctuates this terrain is walking. John is back at work, so I walk with friends, I walk with family, I walk alone. Walking is what persists. I remember that Jess undertook marathon charity walks in the aftermath of her treatment and that power walking along the seafront in the dark now replaces booze-fuelled nights in the pub.

At the time of writing, I notice that walking as a method for overcoming grief is also the premise of the film Evelyn (2018), a film described by Charlie Philips as being "very British – partly for this inability to overcome a stiff upper lip when faced with grief and for its gorgeous landscapes" (Philips: 2018, p.34). In Evelyn, walking in the countryside is portrayed as a cathartic process that humans have always engaged in and the act of walking and getting lost – a dérive – is also celebrated by Sonia Overall as being a potential method for enhancing creativity (2015). In our hour of need, Jess and I choose to follow ancient paths in search of a better sense of ourselves and to guide our personal and creative recoveries.

Figure 3: Red hat

Setting off

Chris

We set off on our walk with a vague plan to walk about 10km in the direction of Chanctonbury Ring. I have brought too much stuff: an old camera, food, water, drawing materials, a notebook – the heaviness of the bag attesting to the fact that this is a walk that has a sense of responsibility and an agenda attached to it, mirroring the weight of emotional and physical baggage we are carrying, but also a sign of my preparedness for this journey of discovery to begin. Jess and I chat, we begin the steep climb from the carpark to the South Downs. Jess slips and slides up the wet muddy path. I have walking boots and am firmer of foot. The same walk but a distinct experience for each of us, thanks to our different footwear.

We stop halfway up the track and pause briefly to notice the mist, the trees and the rivers of water running down the hill, and to take a few photos. I notice a solitary tree slanting awkwardly towards the gravelly path. There is no foliage, its branches bare, a reminder that spring hasn't arrived yet, echoing perhaps how I feel.

I think about drawing a few sketches – instead I just enjoy standing in the woods, staring through the veils of mist at the trees. The conversation is unbounded and intermingled, the gaps and spaces between health, work and family life constantly interrupting any attempt to focus on one aspect and this feels right because all these strands of my life are interwoven rather than singular. We set off again and head in the direction of the Ring. Dense cloud means we can barely see a few feet in front of us. I am glad not to be alone. I am glad we are we.

After a short walk, the trees which make up Chanctonbury Ring appear before us, magically and beautifully. The gentle clouds of mist that veil the trees mirror the fogginess and indistinctness of my own thinking. The place feels dormant, grey and dank, waiting for the sun to break up the mist. There are no signs of spring here, no buds on the trees, just bare branches and soggy moss and barren underfoot. It feels like an achievement. We have enacted an idea; we are here. It is a special place, a prehistoric hill fort that was also used in Roman times as a religious site. The remains of temples are buried deep in the mounds that shape the surface of the Ring. Today it feels ghostly and cold, the atmosphere reminds me of the chill I sometimes experience entering a disused church. I shiver. The place echoes how I feel, and I think about how I might paint this image of greyness.

Maps

> We would all do well to recall these felt maps – for they are
> born of experience and of attention. Such maps, held in the
> mind, are alert to a landscape's changeability as well as its
> fixtures… they offer knowledge that might be found, as it
> were, off-grid.
>
> (Macfarlane: 2018, p.32)

Jess

We make it to the top.

"Do we need a map or anything?" I ask.

Chris laughs at me. "It's impossible to get lost on the Downs."

She has walking boots for Christ's sake. I trust her completely. Early on, the ring itself appears suddenly from out of the thick fog. It's like it's crept up on us despite its enormity: an almost perfect circle of trees that, despite its geometry, maintains a sense of wildness. There is a sense of belonging but no order, as if nature has just decided to be this way. The grass and moss are already lush and green. Spring has sprung from the knee down, but the trees are barren, jet against the light grey mist and jade floor. We perch on a fallen log and talk about what we want out of the day. Chris had made an omelette, but I cheated and went to M&S. The domestic goddess and the fraud break bread. We go over how cancer has left her feeling and her worry about her practice.

"Everyone keeps telling me to paint my way through it, paint how I'm feeling, but I don't want to! I can't."

I talk about cancer too and how that and being a mum and building Creative Writing as a subject at the university from a module to three busy courses has blinkered me, stopped me from really dwelling on what it was like and how it felt to be diagnosed. I tell my students to take risks, to write, to give their creativity the time it deserves but I am a cheat. I write my articles and chapters and edit journals and books but my passion and love for my own practice has been Halal-ed, bled out. And I want it back. I also feel like the busyness of work made it impossible for me to be attentive and tune in to how I was feeling when I was diagnosed. This, and my family willing me to be alright, means I repressed the experience but beneath the trees – finding my way? – I decide I need to write about it, to open the box.

This process of dialogue and collaboration might be the way, as I have a responsibility to Chris to get this book done and it feels right. But I'm still drawn to think of the short way round – a book I can add to the CV, another step closer to being professor – rather than taking my time and writing the right book. It makes me feel sad that there is even this thought in me, but it feels safe out here with Chris to say it aloud into the mist and watch the words get lost in the gloom. *Will they find their way back to me?* Chris challenges me on rushing through everything efficiently but never feeling as though I do anything really well.

"I feel like I'm on a conveyor belt, like I can't stop, like I have to keep going, and if I do stop, it will all fall apart because I'll have to face up to the fact that I'm winging it."

Chris looks at me, bemused, "I've never thought that about you. But I worry you've told yourself you need to be professor and then it will all be ok. What if it's not?"

I realise she is right and I wonder where this quest started and why. I am clambering to be professor but what does that even mean, and won't the pressure intensify when I do? No one has ever told me that the mark of my success will be how old/young I am when I become Professor Moriarty and, right now, my children being happy and me being alive and cancer-free to watch them grow up is all that really matters.

Figure 4: Fork in the road

Which way now?

Jess

The night before our walk, Chris emailed her initial thoughts and I'm reminded how good her writing is. We have written together in the past and she always approached the work with professionalism, getting the words on the page and then taking feedback and developing our articles (Moriarty & Reading, 2012). Her writing is personal and well-researched. She has a sense of story and a clear voice and has been successful getting her work published. She also wrote a huge PhD but refuses to call herself a writer which always interests me.

"But you are," I say. "Couldn't writing be a way back?"

She stops walking for a moment and digests. I watch her hopefully, expectantly. She doesn't love the idea. Before her illness her paintings were bold and bright and instantly remind the viewer of life and humanity. Perhaps writing doesn't have that immediate burn. I don't paint at all and so have nothing to say about toxin-free paints or style, but I do know she can write. I also know that, selfishly, I want her to work on this chapter with me and then on a book we've been mulling over for years about creative practice. I really want to write that book. But is this fair?

She speaks slowly, "I could try."

It isn't quite enough, not yet, but it is a start, and en route we discuss ways that might enliven the process – a second walk and pseudo-writing retreat/ session. This suits me and excites me but it's too safe for her. I like safe. I like deadlines and outputs and knowing things will be done. It's a path I tread with confidence and I'm feeling happy when we come to a fork in the road, but Chris isn't as enthusiastic.

"I'm not sure where we are," she says. "We might be lost."

Two men in Lycra stop their bikes to give us directions. "Good luck girls!" they call good-naturedly as they cycle off.

"I don't want to be told where to go by men," I bristle, but Chris laughs off the patriarchy and we keep going.

Turning around

Chris

I ponder Jess's challenge that I might direct my creativity through writing rather than painting and I wonder if this is possible. For me, painting involves a process of seeing and erasure, a constant reworking that requires a balance between audacity and precision to get it right. A preparedness to allow all to be lost or gained by a single sweep across the surface of the canvas. One gesture that shifts a painting away from having something of its own to convey. I might set out with an intention for the painting, but this is typically set aside for something that arises entirely from the work itself. The painting will be what it will be – an expression of all my individual encounters with the canvas. The difficulty is knowing when the work and I have given all we can, when it is not perfect, but the best conclusion we can offer. Writing for me is tainted by feelings of shame at not being able to pronounce or spell words I want to use and a sense of mangling sentences so that the meaning slips away from what it is I want to say. I feel that I can express myself more eloquently with a single stroke of the brush than I can with 100,000 words. Despite my dyslexia, Jess seems to think that it is possible for me to overturn (or at least lessen) this opinion, so it is my challenge to remain open to that possibility. What can writing say that painting cannot, and vice versa? Painting speaks from an unknown place within me, it is pre-verbal, unconsciously driven. Sometimes I don't even know why I have painted something, but I follow the painting process and know that something will emerge that is of significance to me. Writing feels more present in the world, more direct and accountable. For me there is nothing slippery in writing, whereas painting seems to help my sometimes imprecise and ambiguous ideas to surface. Writing challenges me to name those ideas and present them to the world in a definite form, asking me to stake a claim to knowledge that I refuse to be tied to because I am still wrestling to understand what it is I want to say. So here I must acknowledge that my avoidance of writing also reflects my lack of confidence, not just in its form but also perhaps in my own voice.

We pass a friendly woman on a horse called Treacle and again we check the way.

She echoes the earlier directions. "Take the lower path across the valley, first fork on the left." She makes it sound easy.

We get to the bottom on the hill and take the left fork as directed, the path is marked: *Private property no public right of way*. We hesitate – is this the way? We are uncertain but we decide to plough on despite slight uneasiness generated by the forbidding sign. We walk, we chat as we meander through the vineyard, it is interesting but the closed-off fields and the high fences aren't inviting – surely this is not the way? We retrace our steps to the fork in the road and decide that we took the wrong turn. We walk further up the hill and, as bidden by the men in Lycra and then the woman on the horse, look for another left turn, another gate which is always open, another middle path, with muddled memories of their directions guiding our way.

We set off again. A new path: we have renewed hope. We laugh. Setbacks, dead ends, U-turns are to be expected on the way, a small inconvenience, part of the experience. Except no clear path emerges – just fields with fences. We find ourselves in a field trying to get our bearings. Should we even be here – have we trespassed again? How have we managed to lose the right way? Is Chanctonbury Ring to the left or the right? I have a strong sense that it is on our left and point to a clump of trees. Jess points to an equally convincing clump to the right. I am not sure now.

Panic

Jess

We are lost and the feeling rises like bile in my throat. Gone is the optimism and sense of possibility. Instead, this feels disorganised and badly planned. Where we once celebrated risk and not knowing, now I'm wishing for the order and precision I said I wanted to escape. We talk about completing a sort of circuit that Chris is instinctively sure is wrong, but I don't want to retrace our steps because it feels unnatural, like a sort of defeat. When we started out, it felt like we had all the time in the world to explore and find out, but now the clock is ticking and I can already picture me turning up late at the school and telling my kids, "Mummy was late because she was working," standing there covered in mud and grinning inanely at an equally dubious teacher and set of school-gate mums. It brings up all my guilt about juggling work and family and feeling as if both never get the best of me.

"Let's just go back?" Chris offers as I work myself up into a mild frenzy. "You'll make it."

The desire to keep going is suddenly overridden by my need to be on time when the school bell goes and I concede that Chris is right, we must go back.

Are we still playing it safe and is it my fault? I wonder as we change direction. I'm striding now, we are against the clock and I'm conscious that Chris is still not fully recovered from her operation. The hill is steep, and she gently touches her side. The M&S wrap hasn't settled in my stomach.

"Don't worry Jess; I'm fine, keep going!"

She is typically generous seeing my mounting terror and we push on.

Return

Chris

The walk home is brisker, urgent even. It's uphill, brisk, no stops – conversation set aside. Jess's fear of being late fills the air and I remember that frantic feeling from bringing up my own children. The same walk then, but different – a different experience of the same road. We learn that you can set off in a direction, that there can be a plan or no plan, that there can be dead ends, that trespassing on the space of others is often unintentional and that even with the guidance of others we get lost sometimes. We learn that the feeling of getting lost is uncomfortable, potentially divisive, brings anxiety and tension and that in the end you need to make a call, go back the way you came and be sure of your return or take a riskier unknown path, and that these decisions are influenced by time. We are reminded that it's time-consuming to lose your way because you can never be sure of how long it will take you to find a different way back.

Jess

When you take a path you wanted to avoid, it doesn't have to feel like a defeat. The weather lifts and the view is different from the new perspective. We have walked almost ten miles by the time I slip and Chris ambles down the chalk hill to the car. I'm not late to get the kids, I just make it. I scoop their warm and expectant bodies up in my arms. Later, I write these thoughts down, make sense of the tangle of words and thoughts and directions and try to imagine what is to come.

Reflection on method

Chris

What then is this method? A method that doesn't force me to separate my body from my mind. Whatever Jess and I ultimately name this method, I realise this process has produced a shift in my creativity moving me away from a stuck place in my painting to writing poetry and prose, which I had hitherto regarded as forms I dare not attempt for fear of ridicule or failure. Somehow this simple method of walking and dialogue has produced a change in me, which I would characterise as a willingness to be guided, to venture into the unknown, to write even though I am dyslexic. Ultimately it is about challenging the story I have told myself and been told – of being unable to write and allowing myself to try. I have surprised myself by producing prose and poetry and enjoying the process of doing that. I do not think this means that I will abandon painting for writing but somehow the method has strengthened me and helped me to return to the task of painting with an expanded sense of my own creative repertoire.

This method, through its dialogue with another, brought me into a confrontation with my own creativity in the present moment and created a safe space that allowed the mixed agenda of home, work and health to interweave and to ebb and flow. This is helpful because it allowed me to see that the objectives and goals for my creativity and practice could emerge from this interwoven space and not be formed solely by workplace agendas. I suddenly feel a sense of possibility and expansiveness that has been lost to me and I feel compelled to keep going and see where it takes me.

New phase of making

Jess

When I asked Chris to walk with me and see what happened, it came from a place of desperation: desperation to see my friend working and making again, smiling again. To be the old Chris, my friend and colleague who was always jolly and irreverent and up for a large glass of wine. But she isn't old Chris, she is this Chris, Chris who has had cancer. And there is no going back to who we were, as much as we might sometimes wish to. The process of walking, talking, making, reflecting has helped me come to know Chris again, a little differently, a little better. I have watched her take risks, push herself and talk openly about her fears and hopes. I count myself lucky that this Chris is here. I am blown away by her vivid poetry and moving prose, by the colour and the joy in her new drawings. I am humbled and grateful that she still chooses to call me 'friend'. I hope Chris starts to value the writer I know she is and that we use this method to work with other women also on journeys of recovery – recovery from health issues, expected or unexpected changes, identity shifts – anything that has affected their creativity and made them feel in need of another way of being. I hope we can work together to support each other with mapping those journeys and discovering real and imagined spaces to feel creative along the way. Chris isn't sure, but I know this is something she can start to lead the way on. I feel as if we are packing for a new walk, Chris and I, and that she is more prepared and surer of foot than she knows. I feel as if we have led and followed and pushed and waited when either of us needed to stop, always together, always able to encourage and lift if the other lost their way. We haven't found a way back to who we were before and that's okay. This process has helped us to accept and value the women we are. Women who have had cancer. Women who make. Women who walk.

Chris

For me, the process we have identified is in a dynamic and embodied relationship, its power lying in the stories Jess and I shared, and the trust and support we offered each other during this journey. We brought to these occasions, not just our different experiences of cancer and its impact on our creativity, but also all our histories and our tentative hopes for the future. Our discussions were wide-ranging, not confined to narrow margins but woven between life, work and health, past and present, now and in the future. Our conversations were held and shaped by walking, bringing an awareness of a subjectivity that is in the moving body and the landscape. Surgery meant that cancer had brought a sense of disassociation from my body, an organ removed, a scar to be borne, and walking provided a way to listen to it and re-orientate my sense of self in its aftermath. I realise too that illness brought not just sadness but also self-absorption, a focus on the self, but that my conversations with Jess meant making space for the other and so encouraged an opening up and expansiveness within myself. Creativity needs a balance of relying on the self and focus but also discussion, community – an opening up of ideas and thoughts that we had both lost when we started the project.

At the heart of the method was a willingness to make space for the other and re-engage with my creativity in a form I was fearful of, namely writing. It involved setting aside any concerns about whether what I was doing was any good or not – the point was not to judge but to make the work that I wanted to make in that moment to get my creativity and personal circumstances back in the flow. I used this method to re-find and re-orientate myself, both within the landscape and within myself, to navigate my way to new terrain and a renewed sense of self. Our process acknowledges that the stories and narrative we exchanged were told in fragments and that the meaning and power of the approach emerge as much from what is left unsaid as it does in the overlaps and commonalities of the experiences we talk about.

Our Method

Our new practice is a form of cartography, a map of our own making. The glorious Sussex landscape is our terrain, but walking, talking, reflection and writing are our co-ordinates and so this is a new path. It moves us away from who we were, helps us to recover and gives us time to regroup. We are navigators, explorers, orienteers. Guided by each other and no longer as fearful of where we might be heading – professionally, creatively, and always personally.

The first part of this process was to enter a pact, a mutual contract triggered by a desire by both parties to alter or enliven our creative practice and use this to help our recovery from personal change or crisis. This contract included:

- A timetable that both committed to, with definite start and finish points

- Trust – a willingness to lead and be led on each other's creative journey
- Mutual respect – listening, constructive feedback and equal time on the project
- Openness to change – personal and creative
- Willingness to take risks and resist comfort zones

Figure 5: Memories of a walk

Our work combined a cyclical process of:

- Getting away from conventional workspaces, moving – we chose walking
- Dialogue – purposeful conversation about work, creative process, health
- Writing – about our experience of the walk itself and any stories/memories the process triggered
- Feedback – we read each other's work and gave constructive critique to help with editing and redrafting but also asked questions about what the work might mean.
- Reflection – how had the process made us feel and what had it made us think/write about and why? What had changed and what had stayed the same – emotionally, academically and in relation to creative process and practice?

The method can and will lead to:

- Writing (or other creative practice)
- Reflection on the method, including amendments and developments
- Identifying changes to creative practice(s)
- Personal shift and transformation – feeling differently about an event or circumstance
- The personal and professional relationship being deepened and strengthened
- A clear pathway forward for creative and professional practice

Next Steps: Creative Recovery

This book has been developed by evolving our initial method of walking-talking-making to aid our own creative recovery (Reading & Moriarty, 2019) to identify and learn from strategies that have helped us move through and past stuck places to help us develop tasks that you, the reader, will engage with to shift and transform your own processes. The book is focused around three key concepts:

- Insights into our own experiences of being creatively stuck and our method of recovery
- Reflection – what does our creativity need?
- Creative tasks – activities to reignite your creativity

Each chapter has been organised around a particular structure: a walk, a piece of writing in which we discuss our own creative recovery, and then a task to encourage your own creative shift. Developing the book in this way is a deliberate attempt to extend the feeling of connection and creative support that the original project gave us. We now extend this practice to readers of this book, widening the community to demonstrate that none of us is alone.

A programme of walking

Chris

Jess and I committed to seven walks over a 12-month period. In these walks we agreed to talk about our creativity and how to move it on from the stuck place where it languished post-cancer. We agreed to use these to drive a creative change that would result in content – autobiographical stories – for the book. We completed four walks before the Covid restrictions during lockdown in March 2020 halted the remainder of our planned programme of walks. For a while our project stalled and found itself in its own stuck place as our priorities turned to supporting family and friends and realigning our working lives online. During this time, we walked separately in our own localities talking via headphones about the challenges we were facing daily and although these walks were not really part of the placed programme, nevertheless we did talk and write about this time and our experiences are included in the book to reflect what happened during the process of the research and how our creativity shifted.

The final walks took place during the second lockdown when Jess and I were permitted to walk together. For the sake of family and friends, there were no hugs of greeting and we walked locally, often revisiting a place on the seafront that was equidistant between us and where we had walked before. The final walk took place after the second lockdown ended.

Walk 1. Stanmer Park to Chattri Memorial and back
Walk 2. Brighton Marina to the Palace Pier and back
Walk 3. Chanctonbury Ring: The return
Walk4. Balcombe Circular via Ardingly Reservoir
Walk 5. Covid diaries. Lockdown. Alternatives to walking
Walk 6. Final walk: Devil's Dyke to Ditchling Beacon and back

Creative Tasks for the Reader

In this section, we talk about our own processes of writing and making and the activities that inspired and motivated our own recovery. We reflect on the strategies and experiences that have helped us navigate a time post-cancer and helped us to restore our creativity. The emphasis here is on motivating and moving our creativity, on valuing new and old ways of being creative and seeing them as an essential part of our lives and who we are. Working in this way, we have created an accessible model with a series of creative tasks to support and encourage creativity.

Task

We would like you to begin by reflecting on the questions below. You could write your answers or draw/make a response.

- What is your earliest memory of being creative?

- How did you encourage your creativity or what/who inspired it?
- Do you have an inner critic and how do you work with/against that?
- When and where are you most creative? What are the tools/space/people you need?
- How does it feel when it all comes together and works? Do you have an example?
- What are the things that hinder or demotivate your creativity?
- Can you think of a specific time or event when you hit a wall? (This could be anything – coronavirus, doing a job that was not right, health, a time when your creativity just seemed frozen. It is completely up to you what you choose to share and how personal/practical/professional it is)
- How did you get through/round/past?
- What is the best advice you've had?
- What does your creativity need?
- Where do you hope you will go next with your creativity?

List of Figures

Figure 1. Hope (2019). Watercolour on paper. 26cm x 26cm
Figure 2. Chanctonbury Ring to Winston's Vineyard and back. Pen and ink on paper (2018). 38cm x 28cm
Figure 3. Red hat (2018). Acrylic on board. 20cm x 15cm
Figure 4. Fork in the road (2018). Acrylic on board. 20cm x 15cm
Figure 5. Memories of a walk (2019). Mixed Media on canvas. 92cm x 92cm.

Bibliography

Bakhtin, M. M. (1981) *The Dialogic Imagination. Four essays by M. M. Bakhtin* (Emerson, C. & Holquist, M. (Eds.) Trans. Holquist, M.). Univ. of Texas Press

Barone, T. (2003) 'Challenging the educational imaginary: Issues of form, substance, and quality in film-based research', *Qualitative Inquiry*: 9, 202-207

Clark-Keefe, K. (2002) 'A fine line: Integrating art and fieldwork in the study of self-conceptualisation and educational experiences', *Alberta Journal of Educational Research,* XLVIII (3) 1-27

Eisner, E. (1997) *The Educational Imagination: On the design and evaluation of school programs* (3rd ed.) Macmillan

Ellis, C. & Bochner, A. P. (2000) 'Autoethnography, personal narrative, reflexivity: Researcher as subject' in Denzin, N. & Lincoln, Y. (Eds.) *The Handbook of Qualitative Research* (2nd ed.) pp.733-768, Sage

'Evelyn' (2018) Dir. Orlando von Einsiedel. Violet Films, Grain Media Production

Finley, S. (2003) 'Arts-based approaches to qualitative inquiry', *Qualitative Inquiry*, 9(2):281-296

Hunt, C. (2000) *Therapeutic Dimensions of Autobiography in Creative Writing.* Jessica Kingsley Publishers

Macfarlane, R. (2018) 'Wizards, Moomins and pirates: the magic and mystery of literary maps', *The Guardian*, 22 September. https://bit.ly/creativeA

Moriarty, J. (2014) *Analytical Autoethnodrama: Autobiographed and Researched Experiences with Academic Writing.* Sense Publishing

Moriarty, J. & Reading, C. (2010) 'Helping creative writing and visual practice students to make links between their creative processes and their personal, vocational and academic development', *Journal of Writing in Creative Practice* 3(3) 285-298

_____ (2012) 'Linking creative processes with personal, vocational and academic development in cross-disciplinary workshops', *International Journal for Cross-Disciplinary Subjects in Education (IJCDSE)*, Special Issue, Vol 1 Issue 2. https://bit.ly/creativeD

Overall, S. (2015) 'Walking against the current: generating creative responses to place', *Journal of Writing in Creative Practice*, 8 (1). pp.11-28.

Phillips, C. (2018) 'London film festival 2018: documentaries to watch out for', *The Observer*, 30 September 2018. https://bit.ly/creativeE

Richardson, L. & St. Pierre, E.A. (2005) 'Writing: a method of inquiry' in Denzin, N. & Lincoln, Y. (Eds.), *The Sage Handbook of Qualitative Research.* (3rd ed.) pp. 959-978. Sage.

Saarnivaara, M. (2000) 'The boundary within me: Reflections on the difficulty of transgression', *Auto/Biography* 8(1&2) 56-61

_____ (2003) 'Art as inquiry: The autopsy of an [art] experience', *Qualitative Inquiry* 9, 580-602

Saarnivaara, M. & Saarnivaara, B. (2003) 'At the meeting place of word and picture', *Qualitative Inquiry* 9(4) 515-34

Scott-Hoy, K. (2002) 'The visitor' in Bochner, A.P. & Ellis, C. (Eds.), *Ethnographically Speaking: Autoethnography, literature, and aesthetics* (pp. 274-294). AltaMira Press

_____ (2003) 'Form carries experience: A story of the art and form of knowledge', *Qualitative Inquiry*, 9(2) 268-280

Scott-Hoy, K. & Ellis, C. (2008) 'Wording Pictures: Discovering heartful autoethnography' in *Handbook of the Arts in Qualitative Research: Perspectives, Methodologies, Examples, and Issues* (pp. 127-141). Sage

Slattery, P. (2001) 'The educational researcher as artist working within', *Qualitative Inquiry* 7(3) 370-398

Tierney, W. & Lincoln, Y. (Eds.) (1997) *Representation and the Text: Re-framing the narrative voice.* State University of New York Press

Woolf, V. (1989) *A Room of One's Own*, (Reissue edition). Mariner Books

Chapter 1: Why are we doing this?

Walk 1: Stanmer Park to Chattri Memorial and back

Rain

Chris

The water scalds my frozen skin, but it doesn't matter, I can hardly feel anything, just a distant recognition that the water is way too hot. There is something about being so cold that means I do not feel this intense heat, recognise its danger, its ability to burn. As the blood rises to the surface and comes out of hibernation, my skin itches and I adjust the shower to a more normal temperature, begin to thaw, and enjoy the warm water warming my bones and watching it, slightly mesmerised, drain away down the plughole.

My clothes lie in a pile on the bathroom floor, soaked through. The wind and the rain have penetrated right through to my underwear. Nothing escaped. Even my coat, proper all-weather attire bought on a family holiday in the Lake District, is slumped on the floor like a big damp cotton wool bud: heavy, cold, sodden. The waterproof shoes and thermal socks have not withstood the battering either. They will take days to dry out.

It's raining hard, big glops of water – it's hard to call them raindrops – fall heavily and steadily on the roof of the car as I wait for Jess to arrive. The wind makes the world seem horizontal; trees struggle to retain their natural upright dignity. I turn up the heat; listen to the radio and build a warm damp fug. The sky is an unremitting grey without a glimmer of light; the weather is set for the day. I don't feel like going for a walk. The ordeal of the latest health check has sapped my energies. Secretly, I hope that Jess will agree that the weather is just too awful to walk, and we can retreat to the cosy café instead, look out the window and say *never mind, another day.*

Jess arrives, she springs out of the car, full of bounce, she's waving a book in her hand called *Wintering* (Katherine May, 2020).

"That's what we are doing," she says. "Now is the winter of our discontent."

Certainly, I know I am hunkering down, post-cancer, unsure about how to move forward. We walk around the corner to the café, agreeing that we will have at least one cup of tea before we set off. I have a vain hope that the rain will ease; I am delaying. I secretly hope cake will win.

"We need a metaphor for the book," Jess says, "a symbol that represents what we are doing."

It seems a good idea, a visual or verbal metaphor for the process we are engaged with that will make our ideas accessible to all.

"The water cycle?" Jess suggests.

I like the idea and vaguely remember it from geography lessons at school, cycles of evaporation and deluge feeding into a system of rivers and streams. I don't reply, I'm not sure how it fits, I am digesting the idea, but perhaps Jess is discouraged by my silence and lack of comprehension and adds, "Is it too dispersed?"

"How about a well?" Jess says, "a symbol for going deeper into ourselves, finding signs of life when we were expecting none?"

The idea sticks, we are excited and high five.

"That's it," we say.

In our mind's eye we can see a book on the shelves with the title *Well* emblazoned across it, inviting people to find their own well, to be well. It seems to fit. We relax and flesh out the idea a little. Perhaps we could walk to all the wells in Sussex? But almost as soon as she says it, Jess's face drops: wells are dark, damp scary places that you can fall in and can't get out of, as well (sorry) as being a source of nourishment and hope. I think of the literature that is associated with the notion of the well, "The Well of Loneliness?" I say struggling to remember who wrote it, "Sylvia Plath?" (I found out later it was Radclyffe Hall, 1928). Jess's face falls further. Doubts are mounting, but the idea lingers between us, and we are reluctant to let it go because that would mean we haven't found a metaphor that will steer us through this process.

The rain continues hard.

"We walk no matter what," Jess reminds me.

She seems determined. I set aside my dithering and put my coat back on, swallow the last of the tea and we set off. I am willing to be propelled by Jess's determination and enthusiasm and anyway, as well as my reluctance there is another voice, a deeper voice in me that knows from past experience that walking will lift my mood.

The walk we have planned is a loop of a familiar part of our local countryside, from the car park at Stanmer House, through the woods, onto the open downs towards the Chattri, an Indian war memorial on the South Downs, and back through farmland to Stanmer Park. Not that far, about 9 kilometres, perfectly achievable, enjoyable even, but today the ferocity of wind and the rain changes the familiar landscape into something formidable right from the start.

As we walk, we talk again about the idea that might guide the book, ready now to relinquish the idea of the well as too gloomy by half.

"We need something more positive, more uplifting," says Jess.

I talk about a series of workshops I am doing called *You Belong Amongst the Wildflowers* (Reading, 2020), a series of events about local flora and fauna in Bristol, driven by a commitment to change and regeneration. It is inspired by a piece of embroidery of the same name made by one of the clients – it was on display at last year's art exhibition at the Milestones Trusts charity. I found the work so touching that I bought it and hung it on my bedroom wall.

"What about wildflowers?" I ask.

Jess is interested, she looks at me hopefully, "Better than 'The Well.' More us? It would need to be just one flower, so that we can describe its different stages," she says emphatically.

"A poppy?" I suggest.

"It's been done – too loaded," Jess replies.

We run though a list of options without associations to war or drugs: a daisy is too childlike, too Disney, a wild rose – too thorny! We elaborate. Talk turns to seed pods, a plan to visit Wakehurst Place, and interviews with gardeners about the stages of growth. It seems like a solution, a metaphor for our creativity. We envisage a new book on the shelf with a flower blooming on the front cover, all sunshine and happiness, the process of seedling to flower guiding and structuring our path through the wintering of our creativity to a blooming of it. It's a better fit and we are buoyed up.

"Let's investigate further," we chime.

Figure 6: Wildflower

We walk out of the shelter of the woods headlong into the driving wind and rain onto the Downs, a place that is breezy even on the mildest summer day.

There is not a soul in sight, no dog walkers, no day-trippers. Later, at home, we learn that there was a weather warning covering Sussex, urging people to stay inside and stay safe because of the high winds and pelting rain. After a while, we realise we are not sure of the way and get out our phones, but rainwater has drowned the software that might locate us on the map.

"Put the phone in a bowl of rice when you get home, that's meant to do the trick," Jess suggests, as I look at it despairingly.

In the end, to protect the phones from the driving rain we are forced to bury them in Jess's gloves and place them deep inside her rucksack.

Jess's wellington boots are literally full to the brim with water. She empties them out and, as I watch her do this, I can feel the rain trickling down my back, penetrating the layers of my inadequately waterproofed coat. We plough on with a vague sense of direction towards the Chattri. Having come this far, we are determined to see this sight, to reach our goal.

And then we see it, a sign to the Chattri veering off to the left away from the main path, at least we are heading the right way. And after what seems like an endless walk along a wet stony path, the Chattri emerges in the distance like a beacon, a white building with a small dome and eight pillars. It is a striking sight set against the lush grasslands that surround it.

We pause to admire the building and congratulate ourselves for getting here, taking shelter under nearby trees. It seems fitting somehow that according to the local council, "The Chattri (constructed 1921 and designed by E.C. Henique from Mumbai) means 'umbrella' in Hindu, Punjabi and Urdu and symbolises the protection of the memory of the dead." It is a memorial to Indian soldiers (Hindus and Sikhs) from the First World War who were hospitalised at the Royal Pavilion in Brighton. Those who died were cremated on the downs and the Chattri was built on the same spot. It's surrounded by the South Downs National Park and there is a stillness that surrounds the site, even though the weather is wild and wet. We rest for a few moments reading the names on the memorial, the record of lives lost.

This idea of honouring memory seems to be important, not just for the dead, but it serves as a reminder to Jess and me that our creativity, the things we make or write, are related to our memories and biographical circumstances and that we have learnt through the research with students that mining these sources can support creativity (Moriarty & Reading: 2012).

On the final stretch of the walk across open farmland from the Chattri to Stanmer Park, we can see the woods in the distance like a homing beacon.

"We made it," says Jess, relieved.

Now that we can see the end and have a sense of how far we have left to walk, we relax a little. When we finally get to the trees at Stanmer, we are thankful for the cover after our exposure on boggy farmland. The ground here is drier, making it easier to walk, as if the roots of the surrounding trees have gulped up all the water, prudently storing it for another day. This final stretch feels like coming home. The trees are still in their winter phase, no signs of spring yet, just beautifully gnarled and knotted branches, waiting for the sap to rise, for spring to come, to wear their dazzling new coat of green leaves. I breathe in, refreshed and cleansed by the deluge of rain.

Later on, after my shower and when I feel warmer, I drink tea and look at an old book on wildflowers that I have been using to inspire a series of drawings and paintings I am doing for a work (Stokoe: 1944). A flower, I reflect, is pretty and colourful and easy to love, especially on a bleak day like today, but the textbook reminds me that they are also highly structured organisms with ovaries taking central place in their structure. The American artist Georgia O'Keeffe was of course famous for painting close-ups of flowers as sexually charged, with petals as vulvas (Hassrick: 1997) and I wonder: is this what we want? Perhaps they are too structured, too sexual, too feminine to serve as a metaphor for the recovery of our creative process? I am reluctant to admit it, but another impasse opens, a silence, a gap to be filled.

I text Jess, thinking to myself that her first thought might be the best option: Let's go back to the rain cycle idea?

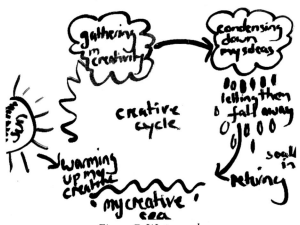

Figure 7: Water cycle

The image of cloud as a repository of creativity, gathering and letting go, seems less colourful but more aligned to the process of creativity itself. I investigate further. I vaguely remember the process from my O-level geography, and I look up a few diagrams of the water cycle on the internet and conclude there is something pleasing about its circularity. A process driven by the sun, in which water from the sea is warmed before being absorbed into the air to form clouds, whose content bursts, and falls, and is soaked into the earth below to replenish the sea. Certainly, I reflect, water is a metaphor for a life as essential as the sun or the air: a reminder that we are connected to nature and its cycles.

Perhaps this is indeed the perfect metaphor because I realise through this that my creativity does indeed need warming up, that first and foremost it needs the sun so that I can leave my wintering behind. And that giving myself time to walk and talk with Jess is one way to do that and that somehow, as a result of this process, my creativity would indeed fall like golden rain – each raindrop a manifestation of all I have absorbed and let fall.

I want there to be mileage in this idea, yet I feel exhausted by my effort to push through it, to make it fit. I let the idea slide away, abandoning it because I am bored with this hunt for the perfect metaphor for creative recovery now, and it feels forced, adrift, contrived, because it's not rooted or connected in any way to what Jess and I are actually doing, which is walking and talking and making. Disappointment again creeps in. There is still a fissure in our plan, but I also remind myself that creative ideas don't always reveal themselves that easily and that patience is required. Jess and I decide to set aside the search for a metaphor and simply get on with our plan. Later that week a painting of pink deer frolicking in the forest emerges, visibly playful and alert, in part inspired by my memory of the walk with Jess. Could this, I wonder, be a metaphor?

Figure 8: I am painting pink deer

Figure 9: We walk no matter what

Reflection on Walk One

Jess and I set off on this walk with the intention of deciding on a metaphor that would neatly illustrate our journey towards creative recovery. In this we were frustrated, but instead of imposing a contrived idea on our project, we decide not to name what we were doing but just sit in that liminal space of being unsure, accepting that our intention to progress with the project and our mutual commitment to understanding what our creativity needs to support its recovery, would eventually guide our way. Creativity needs to make mistakes and to fail in order to flourish, but each time we lose our way, doubt creeps in and we wonder why this space can't be inhabited more comfortably.

On a personal level, the rule Jess set of "we walk no matter what" was tested from the off, with my initial instinct of resistance to walking in the driving rain. But once home, I reflect that I had enjoyed the walk and felt excited by the feelings of possibility and hope that fluttered in my mind like newly startled birds taking flight from a branch of a tree. My imagination awakened, thoughts for drawings and more writing began to tease my thinking and I began to feel that it might indeed be possible for me to break the habit of creative inactivity that I had clung to since my diagnosis. I realised there had been a small but discernible shift in my attitude towards my creative life and that the only way to restore it was to be willing to try new creative activities other than painting. And I noticed, too, that because of the walk I had taken up the challenge laid down by Jess and, however tentatively, had tried something new – to write. In the aftermath of this first walk, writing felt like a new and potent way for me to give form and order to the swirling thoughts in my head, anchoring me to the world. But also, I had taken another leap, made a few tentative sketches and my curiosity had been sparked: could I combine image and text to reflect my experience of the walk and my creative recovery? The "yes" answer gave me a freedom and optimism that I had not experienced for some time. A form of creative hope.

The artist and painter Lynette Yiadom-Boakye says, "I write about the things I can't paint and paint the things I can't write about" (Yiadom-Boakye quoted in Schlieker: 2020, p.22). And, whilst I agree that writing and painting and drawing differ from each other in the forms they offer to represent experience, I find myself curious about how these spaces might be opened up, pressed together, overlapped or juxtaposed through the dialogue between these different forms, and about what this might mean for understanding how to support creative recovery.

Task

Set intentions and share your aspirations for your creativity

Identify a friend willing to engage in the method above. Take your creativity for a series of walks or choose another activity that you are both committed to. Set your intention – what you want out of the dialogues and the activity.

Commit to a time and place, don't cheat and talk about something else or, if you do, remind yourselves why you are doing this.

- What does your creativity need right now?
- What do you discover about yourself and your process?
- What difference does it make to your friendship?
- What now?

Remember: you both must make something that captures the experience – reflection, writing (in any style or genre), art, song, performance – and share this with each other.

It helps to carry a notebook/phone so that you can jot down your ideas and plans during or immediately after the walk. Agree a date and time to exchange your work and make it a priority to give your friend your feedback. Ask them questions about what they have done.

If you are stuck, make a map of the walk or the activity that you have done. Draw/write about what you talked about/what you encountered/what you noticed. How does your account of the activity differ from your friend's?

List of Figures

Bibliography

Brighton & Hove City Council (2021) *The Chattri Memorial,* https://bit.ly/creativeF

Georgia O'Keeffe Museum (2021) About Georgia O'Keeffe, https://bit.ly/creativeH

Hassrick, P. (Ed) (1997). *The Georgia O'Keeffe Museum,* Harry N. Abrams

Hall, R. (1928) *The Well of Loneliness,* Jonathan Cape

Img (2021) 'The Water Cycle', https://bit.ly/creativeJ

May, K. (2020) *Wintering: The power of rest and retreat in difficult times,* Rider

Moriarty, J. & Reading, C. (2012) 'Linking creative processes with personal, vocational and academic development in cross-disciplinary workshops', *International Journal for Cross-Disciplinary Subjects in Education (IJCDSE)*, Special Issue, Vol 1 Issue 2, https://bit.ly/creativeD

Schlieker, A (2020) 'Quiet Fires: The paintings of Lynette Yiadom-Boakye' in Lynette Yiadom-Boakye, *Fly in League with the Night.* Tate Enterprises

Stokoe, W. J. (1944) *The Observer Book of British Wildflowers*, Frederick Warne

Looking back

Writing is also a way of knowing – a method of discovery and analysis. By writing in different ways, we discover new aspects of our topic and our relationship to it. Form and content are inseparable.
(Richardson: 2000, p. 923)

Jess

My family lived in a flat above Sketchley dry cleaners on Edgware High Street. There was a Wimpy opposite, but the smell of fast food was usually overpowered by that of dry cleaning fluid, a scent someone should bottle and sell. Just two floors up from the people and pace of North London, I remember sunlight. We must have had winters and it would have been cold most of the time, but I remember my childhood in terms of summers. Maybe, if we are lucky, most of us do? The kitchen door opened out onto the rooftops with a view over Edgware that made my brother and me think of the scene in Mary Poppins where the chimney sweeps high-kick their way over the city's skyline. Realistically, it was pretty grim. The neighbours had an Alsatian in a cage that they fed leftovers to, and my mum had to get up three flights of stairs with a double buggy and shopping in the days when you still went to the baker, butcher or greengrocer and online shopping wasn't even an idea in someone's head. She had gone back to work part-time, so we used to have a minder called Maureen who was kind and firm and smoked all over us. In July 1982, I said goodbye to Maureen.

It must have been summer, perhaps August, when the memory I recall took place, because we hadn't yet moved round the corner to a terraced house just off the high street. I was sitting at the kitchen table with the door open. The sun was streaming through, hitting the Formica and making everything gleam. My mum took out a yellow and black HB pencil and a stack of dad's old scripts from The Gentle Touch and wrote 'Jessy' at the top of the first page.

"You'll need to do this when you start school," she said.

So, I sat there and copied my name out slowly, getting used to the formality of the pencil and the definite direction I was meant to take. Wanting to please her with my first attempt, wanting to get it right.

"That's really good," she said approvingly.

I don't remember anything else about that day – just my name on that page, over and over again, and wanting the summer to end so I could start school and do more of this writing (Moriarty, 2017).

For me, creativity has always involved a process of looking forward and then back. Scanning my autobiographical experiences for interests that might help me make sense of my work in the present, tugging on the golden threads that link what happened in the past and what I am making now, offers a way of mapping what I know and gives me the confidence to explore what I don't. For me, my creativity needs to be rooted in something I am sure of and given space and time to grow in unfamiliar and unexpected ways to keep it new and stimulating. Working with creative practice students on a research project that Chris and I collaborated on when we first met (Moriarty & Reading, 2009) confirmed that this method of valuing the self as an archive works. Enabling students to make links between their sources of inspiration and the development of their creative practice is difficult; they often find it hard to see how their early creativity might have a profound effect on their present practice. Our project discovered that by providing opportunities for students to identify the things within them that inspired their creativity could improve their confidence and ownership of ideas, leading to an evolved sense of themselves as creative practitioners and enhancing their practice. While carrying out this work and hearing what the students had to say, we realised that our creativity thrived in similar conditions and this book is about valuing yourself as an expert in your own creativity. Even when it seems as if your creativity has run dry, mining the past can often help to tap into a spring that will encourage ideas and practice to flow and flourish again.

Summer

Beanbag before his nose fell off
penny sweets in a paper bag
the 3 Billy Goats Gruff
with all the voices
hot chocolate by the pool
at the Ivy Side Hotel
Yannis cocktail bar, 'this is a tick'
Gandy asleep in the front seat of the Citroen
Butterscotch Angel Delight and Agadoo
'I can see a great big spider,
creeping up on you'
4-inch heels and purple mohair

learning to tie laces
on Jim's right shoe
drawing on the walls at 2am
Nana Liz's cake with glacé cherries
the smell of Simple soap
and a copy of Oink
my parents dancing
their Groovy Kind of Love
Enid Blyton books – the lot in one summer
watching dad play God
almost passing out
patent shoes I wasn't allowed
the exploding Sodastream
our first VHS
Knock Down Ginger on Mead Road,
Dartmoor in the rain, again
Dr and Mrs Cooper in cardies
she'd made
Golder's Green Park
and banana lollies
a wasp sting and
my red dress with the flowers
Father Christmas with black leather gloves
losing Matt at the Zoo
his face when we found him
my first day at school
and not feeling scared.

(Moriarty: 2017)

When Nan was in her 20s, her finger got trapped in a revolving door. The pain was so bad that she passed out as the door kept circling. Coming to in Kilburn hospital, she refused to have it reset. As a result, it always pointed at a funny angle so that when she was waggling a finger at you, usually because you'd done something to annoy her, it always looked as though she was pointing at the person next to you. This made it quite hard to take her seriously, even when she was telling you off in her animated Irish bark that might otherwise have stripped flesh from bone. In four-inch heels and decked in purple mohair, Helena Rubinstein lipstick no.12 and masses of green eye shadow, Nan was a sight to behold. Despite being 5 foot 2, even in the heels, her flaming red hair and clouds of Armani perfume made her unmissable on

35

the Jubilee line, travelling from Wembley to work at Dickins & Jones or Harrods or another colossal department store where she was always one of the best sellers of designer clothing to designer women. She was so good at making money for these shops that managers would turn a blind eye to her long lunches and the discreet pilfering by Nan and her mates that meant they were as fashionable and formidable as any of the women they served. They worked hard, and would reward themselves with frequent nights out, piling into black cabs and heading to where the party was at – which was always where they were.

Growing up, I used to admire them so much, these women who looked like something out of Dynasty, had their own money, and knew how to enjoy themselves. Even on the estate where Nan lived, her door was nearly always open, and the neighbours would pop in for a morning mug of tea and a Silk Cut while they gossiped about what was occurring beyond the net curtains. When Granddad was alive, he was often beside himself at her escapades and regular trips abroad on women-only holidays. Her bag was never unpacked and there would always be some aunt or friend who wanted a companion to Malaga or Alicante and Nana May's passport refused to gather dust in a drawer. She wanted to be off and out.

"You've got to make the best of it," she would say, raising a cut glass tumbler of whiskey to the skies as she detailed another trip where the barman just happened to know this secret beach, or the manager had given her a free parasail, or where everyone at the resort's best restaurant all cheered "May!" whenever she walked in.

It had taken my granddad, Jim, three attempts to get my Nan into church. The first two times, she told the driver to circle round and changed her mind but by the third time, her father told her enough was enough.

"On our wedding night, your grandfather stayed up all night drinking with your Uncle Danny and I slept at the end of the bed," she told me. "I just lay there thinking to meself, 'what have you done May?'"

They were a regular Burton and Taylor. Either madly in love or just mad.

It took me three engagements before I would actually marry someone and when I did, he had to organise the wedding or else I swore I wouldn't say "I do." Nan wasn't there when I did, and I don't think she would have approved of the registry office, but she would have loved my black wedding dress, gold shoes and the reception with a free bar.

My grandparents always bought my brother and me expensive toys and took us to the cinema or the drive-thru when they babysat. We would be high on Mary Poppins and sweets by the time they took us home in Jim's red Rover. I never wanted to go to bed when we slept at theirs, but they didn't mind me staying up and watching late night films like Jaws and Dirty Harry. Nan would make me turn away in the scary bits but even now I'm still terrified of swimming in the sea. One night, whilst she painted her nails, Jim taught me to tie my laces on his right shoe and when I finally got it, they both cheered and clapped so she smudged them. She didn't care. Much. She hated a naked finger or toe, and my nails are usually a garish tangerine or green as a tribute.

When Jim died, Nan started taking half a sleeping tablet every night to get her through to morning. She moved into the middle of their huge bed with satin sheets and kept his photo in every room, so she could talk or row with him when it suited her. Several of her exes appeared on the scene and wined and dined her, taking her on expensive holidays and offering to be husband number two (I still have an engagement ring one of them refused to take back in case she changed her mind). She always had more than one beau on the go, and she was always out pulling the strings of Fred or Mac or Alfredo and then letting them go when she got bored.

"I'll never get married again. I swear to you now."

Not that we would have minded, but she was happy to pick them up and let them down as it suited and kept partying with her friends all the while.

Nan was a terrible hypochondriac but lived through the triple bypass and ignored all protestations to stop smoking and drinking. She thought a Chinese take away was a healthy meal and that cups of tea stopped when the bar opened at midday (although with the bad hangovers, sometimes the bar opened at 9am). Before she went down to surgery to have a pacemaker fitted, the anaesthetist had to wrestle her blue make-up bag from her as she tried to put on mascara – with no mirror.

"If I go, I want to have my eyes on at least!" she told him.

"Mrs Moriarty, the only place you are going is to the operating theatre and they don't care what you look like down there." But he relented and let her have a smudge of eye liner, just in case.

When she died, she was in her 80s. Only my Great Auntie Ann knew her real age for sure. She was pulling on a pair of pink knickers and that heart of hers gave in. That heart that loved as ferociously as any I've ever known. If she liked you, at least. If she didn't, it was catty and cold, but I was always in her sun. Maybe she saw in me something of herself that had been filtered through my parents' DNA? Something more measured, less wild, but reckless and burning, nonetheless. I see her in my own daughter, in Arla who at only 9 is bold and has to be who she is, on her terms. Her two brothers are softer, kinder, in awe of her power and her 'nothing will stop me' attitude. Her teachers have told us we need to be stricter with her.

"She's just so feisty," one lamented at a parent's evening.

"That's how we like her," I said.

"Well yes," said the teacher, "but she has to know the world doesn't belong to her."

My daughter waggles her finger and the puts lipstick on without a mirror. She can be the life and soul, but she can cut you dead. She laughs at her own jokes and claps her hands when she does it. She keeps her dad and her brothers on strings she has already mastered. She wants to run for president with the best hair accessories she can find.

I tell her about her great grandmother who wouldn't be tamed, who spoke her mind and loved like a cyclone, lifting you up and up and destroying anything that got in the way. I tell her she was neither just good nor just bad and certainly never in-between. I tell her Nana May would have thought she was the business – that you can never be too feisty if the world's going to belong to you.

So, why am I telling you this? What do the stories about my childhood and feeling almost haunted by my Nan in the expressions my daughter pulls tell you about me and my creativity? What do they tell you about the purpose of this book? My connection to my creativity has been lost at times when I felt I didn't know. I didn't know how to be after I had cancer. I didn't know what stories I wanted to write when my Nan died or when I struggled – still struggle – to juggle being a mum and an academic, even though I knew I needed to be both and that my identity was bound to both. In these periods when the connection was lost, my sense of self faded too and I didn't trust my creative self to find a way back or past these feelings of loss, frustration, sadness, panic. If the structure in my creative practice faltered, I focused on the foundations and where my creativity came from and tried to make these strong but also new to me again. By remembering stories of my past – and the people who inspired and encouraged my creativity – and then using my writing practice to deepen my connections with those stories, I was able to breathe life into my writing again. These stories are about who I am and where I come from and whilst they are not always happy and safe, they remind me of my place in the world, of what I know to be true and why the telling and sharing of stories matters so much to me.

Chris and I suggest that whatever the source, identifying techniques and ideas that inspire our processes and giving ourselves dedicated time and space to develop our creativity will always challenge and therefore develop our creative work. We hope this book will suggest ways of digging into your past and mapping your creativity, and that when combined with the tasks in the book, will help you navigate a way forward and enrich or reignite your creativity.

Nurturing creativity is a very personal act and for this reason it is connected to our intrinsic motivations for learning. Opportunities to reflect on our creativity and how it is embedded in our autobiographical experiences can therefore help us to move through liminal spaces when our creativity seems stunted and stuck. We believe that creativity needs a combination of autobiographical knowing and also seeing what Reid and Petocz (2004) identify as the "detail of the subject, to formulate and solve problems, to see connectedness between diverse areas, to take in new ideas, and to include the element of surprise in their work." If this book doesn't inspire you to try new things and take risks with your creativity, whilst valuing and celebrating what was there in the first place, then it hasn't done its job.

With this in mind, we ask you to set yourself a creative challenge, completing a project that has been set to one side, beginning a new one, trying a different form or technique that will shift your work – and reflecting on your early experiences of being creative to see where the golden threads meet, connect, break.

Task

What is your earliest memory of being creative? Draw, record or write this down and consider how it is connected to your creativity now.

The confidence and belief in our own ideas and our ability to execute them is important for creativity. We all vary in degrees of confidence, which can be eroded by negative criticism, difficult life experiences and a lack of time, but can be supported by engaging in specific tasks and encouragement from peers, family or friends. The key to getting the best out of this book lies in developing a better sense of yourself as a creative person, a person with ideas and things to say via their creative work.

Why not try a list poem similar to the one I have written earlier in this chapter? Write a list of autobiographical details without explaining them or justifying them or revealing feelings. Just document the events and experiences that stand out. You might like to think in terms of a favourite toy, holiday destination, smell that reminds you of someone, a song, an object from that time, a favourite meal, a film, a room in someone's house, a family saying, a political event, but come up with your own too!

Your creativity is supported through engagement with other creative work.

Regardless of our disciplinary focus, writing, drawing, and reading are key skills for creativity. Committing to use these skills interchangeably and using reading and writing to inspire visual practice and also using visual practice to inspire writing will help you to refine and shift your process (Biggs: 2003).

Creativity is hard, it is exhilarating, it matters. In all the stuck places I have found myself in, I was pushed on and up by the teachers, peers, friends and family who understood this. Writing – my own creative discipline and passion – offers me the up-close intimacy with my lived experiences and the necessary detachment that is needed when seeking a viewpoint from which to examine my life. This distance can provide a compelling space from which to review, reflect and revise and offers powerful insight into one's own identity. I would heartily recommend it to anyone starting a creative project. My experience is that this process can offer a method for authenticating self-image and recovering feelings of self-worth, allowing for a more expansive and liberated self that is able to critique and also resist the pressures our creativity might have suffered from. I agree with Hunt (2000) that for some, "where the imagination sets to work on the raw material of the unconscious and turns it into art… engaging with their inner world has a strong self-developmental or therapeutic dimension." The process can be transformational, positive, liberating. Creating can help us to legitimise and value our experiences, to reconnect with who we are and where we have been.

Chris and I suggest that individual creative process is inextricably linked to personal meaning-making and self-knowledge. By giving yourself permission to identify and reflect on your personal motivations for your practice, and what works and what hinders your process, there is an opportunity for you to make this book meaningful and relevant to the development and/or recovery of your own creative practice. Use this chapter to celebrate who you are and what you already know. Use your practice to reconnect or reawaken those connections so you can move forward whilst being surer of where you've been and how it can help you expand your creativity.

Bibliography

Biggs, J. (2003) *Teaching for Quality Learning at University*. Open University Press

Biggs, M. & Buchler, D. (2008) 'Eight criteria for practice-based research in the creative and cultural industries.' *Art, Design and Communication in Higher Education.* 7(1): 5-17

Clegg, P. (2008) 'Creativity and critical thinking in the globalised university', *Innovations in Education and Teaching International*, Vol 45, 3; pp.209-218

Danvers, J. (2003) 'Towards a radical pedagogy: Provisional notes on learning and teaching in art & design', *International Journal of Art & Design Education*, 22 (1): 47-57

Dillon, P. (2008) 'Pedagogy of connection and boundary crossings: Methodological and epistemological transactions in working across and between disciplines.' *Innovations in Education and Teaching International*, Vol 45 (3): 255-262

Dineen R. & Collins, E. (2004) 'Mind the gap: The promotion of creativity in art and design education', *Enhancing Curricula*, 249-266

Dineen, R., Samuel, E. & Livesey, K. (2005) 'The promotion of creativity in learners: Theory and practice', *Art, Design & Communication*, 4(3): 115-173

Harvey, L. (2000). 'The relationship between Higher Education and employment', *Tertiary Education and Management*, Volume 6(1): 3-17

Hunt, C. (2000) *Therapeutic Dimensions of Autobiography in Creative Writing*, Jessica Kingsley Publishers

James, A. (2004) 'Autobiography and narrative in personal development planning in the creative arts.' *Art Design and Communication in Higher Education*, 3(2): 103-118

McWilliam, E. (2007) 'Is Creativity Teachable? Conceptualising the creativity/pedagogy relationship in Higher Education'. *Research and Development in Higher Education* Vol 30 (2): 376-383

Moriarty, J. (2017) 'Soaring and tumbling: An autoethnography from Higher Education'. In Hayler, M. & Moriarty, J. (Eds.), *Self-Narrative and Pedagogy: Stories of experience within teaching and learning* (pp.135-146). Sense

Moriarty, J. & Adamson, R. (2019) 'Storying the self: Autobiographical pedagogy in undergraduate Creative Writing teaching.' *Journal of Writing in Creative Practice*, 12(1-2), 3-7

Moriarty, J. & Reading, C. J. (2009) 'Linking creative practice to the Personal Development Agenda' in *Dialogues in Art and Design: Promoting and Sharing Excellence* (pp. 64-69).

Reid, A. & Petocz, P. (2004) 'Learning Domains and the process of creativity'. *The Australian Educational Researcher*, 31(2)

Richardson, L. (1997) *Fields of Play: Constructing an academic life*. Rutgers University Press

Chapter 2: Accepting Fear

Walk 2: Brighton Marina to the Palace Pier and back

This chapter interweaves Chris and Jess's voices. Jess's narrative is in italics to distinguish between them.

"This is mad."

It's a bleak night, it's already dark and the rain is pelting against the windscreen of my car as I drive over the hill and past the cemetery to meet Jess at Brighton Marina, an agreed halfway point between our homes. There is something both insistent and yet soothing about the rain as it obscures my vision, despite the swishing and swooshing of the windscreen wipers. I am mesmerised by the regularity of this mechanical action and vaguely wonder how I might incorporate this swishing action into my painting, imagining mimicking this jerky action in large regular brush strokes across the canvas. I store away the thought for another day. An obvious metaphor passes through my mind, *there will be tears*, the rain seems to say, *but they can be wiped away* and I laugh to myself at the blunt association I have made, but given that my father-in-law died the day before, it seems appropriate. I am feeling tetchy, sad, and confused about how to grieve for a man who managed that rare feat of dying peacefully in his own home at the age of 95 after a long, happy and successful life. There are memories that push through: small, unexpected stabs of emotion that penetrate my being, as if there is a slow running computer script in the background of my brain that prevents me from functioning properly. But I am fine, just a bit sad as I arrive bang on time at the car park.

Figure 10: Seafront walk 1/7

A brilliant green neon light glows in the dark. Asda is in full swing with shoppers seeking solace and sustenance by filling up their empty trolleys with its perishable goods. A sense of anticipation seems to accompany the flurry of shoppers, a feeling that they will go home with what they want, what they need to guard them from this dark night. I recognise that feeling. I see Jess dressed in the customary uniform we have adopted of leggings, bobble hat and trainers. She waves. I am buoyed. This seems to be a less ridiculous thing to do than it did on the drive over. It's even stopped raining.

Figure 11: Seafront walk 2/7

The rain has been lashing down for hours with severe weather warnings issued in parts of the country. I scour the car park, looking for Chris, wondering if she's had second thoughts.

And then there she is, waving with both arms, also in a bobble hat and leggings, smiling. And I half jog over to her, noticing that the rain has stopped, realising the clouds are starting to part, and that it isn't as dark as I thought it was.

"Glad to see you're looking equally glamorous." She grins and slams the car door shut.

"Come on, let's do this."

We go no matter what. Her rule at first, now ours. I knew she would be here. It's busy now, people braving the storm to do a Monday night shop. The clang of shopping trolleys and cars reversing and revving don't quite silence the South Coast gales. I pivot on my wet trainers, catching the eyes of strangers who look hurriedly away at this manic woman in Lycra. I am tired but also wired. I cannot remember the last time I felt relaxed: it's been a busy weekend with my daughter's birthday party and parents' anniversary, both of which demanded my time and deserved effort. Today, I was teaching and working on a funding bid when a tutor failed to turn up for students on my course and I ended up sprinting round the building trying to find the absent professor and then apologising to disappointed first years. After that I met a PhD student who needs pushing and nurturing. They were tearful and overwhelmed. I know how they feel. This was a pretty typical working day, at the end of which I broke every speed limit to pick two of my children up from drama, get them home and listen to them read before their dad took them to guitar lessons. They looked tired and I felt guilty, bundling them out the door into the night to practise when they probably needed to be in the warm, eating something hot. But I'd told Chris I would do this. I want to do this. When we started the walking to recover project, it helped me accept myself as a woman who has had cancer and now, I want to discover how other artists have recovered, and I need to recover myself, find time and space to tune in to others, learn from them, breathe.

Figure 12. Seafront walk 3/7

We stride though the dark towards the concrete tunnel that will take us to the seafront road and on to the Pier. Our pace is fast, urgent. Despite the rain, it's mild and just a little soggy underfoot. There is a sense that we are both running away from our day as fast as we can, shaking off our lethargy with each step, moving together towards something, towards ourselves? As we walk, I am aware of the regular pounding of our trainers against the tarmac, a pulse as essential to our being as a heartbeat. Set against this is the noise of our chatter, mainly about personal matters, my bereavement and how the family is coping, and Jess's week, a colourful mix of family celebration and recriminations.

Can I find time to breathe?

And we bounce off towards the seafront, out of the concrete and cars and neon lights of Asda, and head in the direction of the Palace Pier, twinkling and shimmering about a mile and half ahead.

Figure 13. Seafront walk 4/7

Along the seafront path, there is hardly anybody about and it is poorly lit. A man walks past, with his hood pulled down over his head against the night, his face unseen. Jess offers a cheery hello but there is no reply. There is a sense of unease. We brush off this failure to receive an acknowledgement from a smiley jogger and head on towards the pier. On our route we walk past a bin and hear a scurrying noise, a rat perhaps, looking to replenish his own supplies, meet his own needs. We shudder as the night seems to bring unseen forces that reach into our bones, creep into our flesh. These feelings of unease are compounded once we arrive at the eerie-feeling pier. It is closing for the night, and we are alone amongst the empty dodgems, the Hotel of Horrors, the silent carousel of horses, the smell of old doughnut fat. Until now the chat has been about our personal lives, but somehow this atmosphere shifts the conversation and propels us to move on, to focus on work, to talk about the project and the work that we need to do.

Figure 14. Seafront walk 5/7

Figure 15: Seafront walk 6/7

As we arrive back at the car park, I reflect that I would not have done this walk alone, I would have felt unsafe, scared of walking past an unknown stranger in the dark, of the ghostly phantoms haunting the empty funfair on the pier, perturbed by the scurrying of the rat, but walking with Jess on this wet blustery evening it feels okay and it's the same perhaps for this journey of discovery we have embarked on in relation to our creativity – a journey I might not make alone but, supported by another, undertake more bravely.

Figure 16. Seafront walk 7/7

Reflection. Life and creativity/Dyads not nomads?

Walking and talking is the way that Jess and I communicate. It is central to our collaborative process, and I think we would find it impossible now not to work in this way. Through these conversations we link our creativity to our everyday lives, to our work, to our friends, to our families, and try to make sense of these disparate but interconnected parts.

Figure 17: Seafront walk – Jess

At the start of any walk, Jess would invariably ask, "How's the family?" and I might follow with, "How's work?" I reflect on this process of checking in with each other, of tuning in to each other's lives, as essential to our method. This journey we have embarked on is about shifting our dominant view of ourselves, a view that has been governed by cancer, and move on and past these experiences to tell other stories about who we are, who we want to become, and where our creativity is in relation to these evolving stories.

We arrived at the start of the walk tired and full of concerns about family and work, with little time or desire to talk about our creativity and this initially felt unsatisfying, but it was a reminder that our creativity coexists with the rest of our lives and sometimes gets squeezed by these demands. For me, this situation is sometimes made worse by an outdated notion of creativity that is fossilised in my head: that it is the preserve of a talented few and is only worth doing if you have the time and the capability to produce something, new, impressive, or monumental. This view of creativity is especially unhelpful because when you feel stuck, what's needed more than anything else is the encouragement and support simply to have a go in whatever way you can manage within the context of your life. The point is not to make praiseworthy pieces of art but simply to make, to write and see what happens, not wait for the ideal time, space, or situation.

By walking, it's as if we set ourselves a direction, a course which is an active demonstration of our desire to move our creativity forward one step at a time. The programme of walks and small specific exercises that we undertake (and offer the reader) provide manageable activities that offer a way of keeping creativity at the centre of life regardless of family and work demands. The walk reminds me that this project is something that we are doing together, and that the creativity of each of us, and the project we are working on together, benefits from working within this dyadic framework because of the support we offer one another.

As we walk, we feed our creativity with the sights, thoughts, sounds and smells of our chosen walk, on this occasion the eerie semi-derelict and industrial landscape that runs between Brighton Marina and the Palace Pier, a walk that spooks us but which, by walking together, we find the nerve to complete.

Task

At the end of the walk, we decided to do the following activities. Why not try all or some of them yourself?

- Write about your physical experience of moving – we have chosen walking but you could choose dancing, playing any sport or just stretching
- Draw where this activity takes place
- How does this connection between your movement and body and your creativity make you feel? What do you notice?

List of Figures

Our Personal Creativity

Jess

Magic Clouds

In earlier research, I argued that writing is best considered as an arts-based practice where students are:

- *Extending and developing creative communities*
- *Acquiring entrepreneurial skills*
- *Building confidence with individual and shared creative tasks*
- *Engaging with work-based scenarios*
- *Developing writing skills in a variety of genres*

(Ashmore & Moriarty: 2015)

I used this definition in the context of teaching creative writing to undergraduate and postgraduate students at the University of Brighton where I initiated the subject and now lead on several creative writing courses, but it is also relevant to my own creative practice which I identify as:

- Connected to the social world
- For publication
- Developing my sense of self as a writer/maker/artist
- In dialogue with colleagues/community partners
- A mix of critical and creative work in a variety of genres

But if these are the key components that I employ to support creativity in my students and in myself, what is creativity? I've never actually tied down my definition of creativity, seeing it as an amorphous magic cloud you can never quite hold or catch, but what makes up the flesh on these bullet-pointed bones?

Creativity is the process of bringing something new into being. Creativity requires passion and commitment. It brings to our awareness what was previously hidden and points to new life. The experience is one of heightened consciousness: ecstasy (May: 1959).

Creativity is rarely ecstasy. Not for me. There is no chemical high or orgasmic release. It rarely feels just organic or just intuitive and, when it does, I don't trust it; instead, I doubt its value and what it might mean to anyone, including me. I have to work incredibly hard at being creative, check that I don't rely on simply regurgitating old ideas without innovating and evolving, whilst also trusting myself, my skills, knowledge and experiences, and also my ability to produce. I have to research (a lot) and I need critique, support and inspiration from my community (a lot). Creativity begins with the self, with me, but in order to evolve and flourish, it has to be in dialogue, collaborative, connected, whether with a reader, or audience, or collaborator, or specific space, or notion. Like Daniel Charney, I believe that "full knowledge cannot be transferred solely through the sharing of information; it must be kept alive and passed on through the experience of making" (Charney: 2011). This is why the process of walking, dialogue and producing is the focus of this book. It's a process we devised and piloted to help us with our creative recovery from cancer (Reading & Moriarty: 2019). Marina Orsini-Jones (2008) argues that "to enable students to cross thresholds it is necessary to devise student-centred activities that allow them to engage both in individual and collective reflection on the troublesome knowledge encountered" (Orsini-Jones: 2008, p.20). Chris and I decided that this could also be applied to our ambition to reboot and adjust our creative practice after feeling lost when we had cancer. The process we devised – Autoethnographic Cartography – helped us find a new way (Reading & Moriarty: 2019).

The method can and will lead to:

- Writing (or other creative practice)
- Reflection on the method, including amendments and developments
- Identifying changes to our creative practice(s)
- Personal shift and transformation – feeling differently about an event or circumstance
- The personal and professional relationship being deepened and strengthened
- Clear pathway forward for creative and professional practice

Chris

In what ways can this method that we have designed be viewed as creative?

Within existing literature there is extensive debate about whether creativity resides in "the person, a process or an outcome" (Dineen et al: 2005, p.156). Jess and I would suggest it is all three and certainly the method we employ within this book values the personal, the practical and the output equally.

According to Donald MacKinnon (1970) and Ross Mooney (1963), creativity consists of four key components:

- the creative product
- the creative process
- the creative person
- the creative situation

When I think about being creative, I think about painting and making paintings that are personal and meaningful to me in some way; that they are of something that matters to me, such as a painting of a family member, or the walks I have done with Jess. Often, it is an effort to portray a mood or a feeling associated with the subject matter I have selected. But I also think about the painting being made in a way and painted in a manner that I am totally happy with, proud of, excited by; then I feel creative, joyful.

Of course, a fierce inner critic means that these elements of a painting rarely come together in a way that I am totally happy with, but for me being creative in my painting practice is also about the struggle to find the perfect balance between the ideas/feeling I wish to convey and the way I have made the painting in terms of, for instance, the marks I make, the colour I use, the scale or media I choose. If I believe any of these elements of the painting is out of kilter, its lack of coherence jars, and the painting remains unsatisfactory, unfinished, leaving me frustrated at my inability to bring it together and making me feel despondent, wooden and uncreative.

There is rarely a straightforward relationship between what I want to paint and how I paint it. I have learnt through the experience of painting that the process of making inevitably imposes its own internal logic that nearly always takes me away from my plan, and that I only truly find out what I want to paint by painting, by spending endless hours in front of the canvas applying, wiping and reapplying paint, to see what emerges from the interaction between my initial plan or thought or the painting and the process itself. For me, creativity is about tuning into this interaction, overcoming my reluctance to discard ideas or processes that aren't working and to listen to, and learn from, what is actually happening on the canvas. Sometimes – quite suddenly – after spending long stretches of time struggling with the paint, a picture emerges that feels right, as if it has been there all along and my job was simply to uncover it (You Can't Tell by Looking, 2020). There are hard-won moments of creative joy. When I do make a painting that gives me a glimmer of a successful outcome, it's a delight, a eureka moment, a soaring of the soul, a moment when I am totally carried away by the process and feel like I am flying. Creativity is about staying flexible, open and willing to change, and remembering that these discarded ideas or processes are never totally lost because in my work the original plan for the painting hovers like a ghost in the background of the finished work, a trace of initial marks now painted over. Metaphorically too, these remnants provide a reminder of the seedbed or initial thoughts or plan that generated the painting. The final painting is an image that is related to the original idea but is not the same as it; rather, it is transformed and made different through the action of making.

It can be delightful and uplifting to produce something that comes from me that then has meaning for others. I remember I made some paintings of my daughter playing rugby, Amazonians running around the muddy windy pitch in the local club colours of maroon and blue. They were painted for my daughter, to show my pride in what she had achieved in her sport. I always worried about her involvement in what could sometimes be a rough game but spending time painting these images helped me appreciate the sense of fun and camaraderie that the game offered her, so I came to understand her motivations for playing a little better. Displaying them in my studio space at the time, a fellow artist was delighted to see the club colours, the club her son played for too. Perhaps there was a shared recognition of the challenges and delights of being a parent, but after seeing my colleague's delight in the paintings, I valued them more, saw them more clearly.

For me, being creative also means making time to soak up and learn from the work of other artists. On a sunny autumn day in October 2020, I make a trip to Blenheim Place to see the paintings of British-born Cecily Brown, whose work I admire. Brown offers a critique of the often-romanticised British heritage by making works in response to the collections at Blenheim. The source materials for her paintings are displayed in a large vitrine in the Great Hall. They include imagery from her childhood in 1970s England such as the album cover for the Beatles' Yellow Submarine, Beano comics, Donald Duck and fairy-story books. These personal items sit alongside her favourite images from art history and drawings she has made of objects in the stately home. She uses this personal combination of reference material to inspire her paintings. As I walk around, I count 12 paintings hung in the various state rooms competing for attention with the historical paintings also on display. For me the most interesting of these paintings is titled *Homage to Reynolds* (2020), hung in the Red Drawing Room, which involves a process of printing a copy of Reynolds' 1777-78 painting *The 4th Duke of Marlborough and his Family* onto canvas and then painting into it to obliterate the image of the duke and his wife and to refocus the painting on Lady Caroline, their eldest daughter and an accomplished painter. This intervention allows Lady Caroline to take centre stage, and the economy of means, in terms of overpainting a digital version of the original, makes the painting effective and innovative, not just in terms of idea, but also in process. It is this play that I find persuasive, creative, in part because Brown shows us something new, something hidden in the depths of this old masterpiece, that gives us another way of viewing it.

Estelle Barrett and Barbara Bolt offer a series of compelling readings about different forms of creative inquiry and make the case for creativity as a process of personal research in which knowledge is: "gained through the relationship of the ideas in the research to antecedent ideas and practices but also from the particularities of lived experiences and living bodies and that this has a capacity to change knowledge" (Barrett & Bolt: 2009, p.138).

In this definition, creative practice and its associative methods are rooted in the practical and the experimental and add to the existing body of knowledge in ways that reflect the lived experience of the artist and "in staging itself as artwork, the particularity of the lived experience is returned to the universal" (ibid, p.140). From this perspective, artists uncover knowledge through the practical process of making, and this is embedded in the processes they use and the artworks they make, resulting in new insights and understandings arising from their involvement with materials, processes, and ideas of practice.

I find this argument compelling because it recognises that the person is at the heart of the creative process and that the process of making has the capacity to generate new knowledge with the objects that are made embodying this in some way. This is important because it means that being creative – whether through writing or making – has the capacity to generate new knowledge, to show us something and to offer us new insights that we didn't see before. Being creative matters.

Task

> *I am the colour of wine, of tinta. The inside of my powerful right claw is saffron-yellow. See, I see it now; I wave it like a flag. I am dapper and elegant; I move with great precision, cleverly managing all my smaller yellow claws. I believe in the oblique, the indirect approach, and I keep my feelings to myself. But on this strange, smooth surface I am making too much noise. I wasn't meant for this.*
>
> (Extract from 'Strayed Crab' by Elizabeth Bishop)

Tedlock (2000) argues that "women's ethnographic and autobiographical intentions are often powered by the motive to convince readers of the author's self-worth, to clarify and authenticate their self-images" (p.268) and identifies this as a feminist issue. In earlier research, I (Jess) argued that a process of storying oneself can offer the necessary detachment that is needed when seeking a viewpoint from which to examine one's lived experiences. This distance can provide a space for reflection that can trigger meaning-making and offer powerful insight into one's own identity (Moriarty, 2017). My experience is that this process can offer artists a method for authenticating self-image and recovering feelings of self-worth, allowing for a more expansive and liberated self that is able to progress their creativity. I agree with Celia Hunt that for some women, "where the imagination sets to work on the raw material of the unconscious and turns it into art… engaging with their inner world has a strong self-developmental or therapeutic dimension" (Hunt: 2000, p.40) and suggest that the process can be transformational, positive, liberating.

In 'Strayed Crab', Elizabeth Bishop gives a scared and lonely crab human characteristics so that the reader understands them as a more complex creature and empathises with their experience of feeling overwhelmed. In this task, you will need to identify an animal that resonates with you. I hope mine is a cat but it's actually a tortoise.

Now paint, draw or write yourself as this animal considering the following things:

- What colour are you? You do not have to be your colour in nature, you might be a red shark or purple tiger.
- Where do you live, and do you like it there?
- What do you eat, and does it give you pleasure?
- What is your biggest fear or threat?
- What brings you joy?
- When you sleep at night, what do you dream of?
- Focus on one aspect of your body. What is it saying, what does it need?
- Where are you going, and will it be okay?
- What is the title of this piece and what does it say about you?

Carapace

I am the colour of rope,
I push myself into the corner of this hutch
Making it hard for hands to snatch and grab me.
The hay is home but not home,

I chew and chew but it sticks
In my stretched neck.
Sometimes, I make it to the end of the lawn,
Onto the soil and press beak to boundary,
Searching for a weakness,
A possible means of escape.
They feed me lettuce and laugh when I
Snap.
Snap.
There is a man who smells like dust
Always putting me back,
Always telling me I must not go further
Than I know I can.
I soak up light and heat, smile at the sun
But at night I dream of somewhere
Warmer than this where the sun spreads through me
And I think, yes, this is me.
When I wake, my eyelids lift
Slowly.
Slowly.
I imagine racing over grass,
Breaking through
A hole   in the fence
Just my size.

Figure 18: Shoot

Shoot (by Chris Reading)

Huntress or protector points her arrow
Freeze
Be still
Look and listen
For signs and clues
Which way should I run, which way should I turn?
Right now, I am in plain sight.
A dangerous moment
Panic
Fright
But if I keep silent, and alert
Perhaps I will not be seen
I watch and I listen
It's my best defence

List of Figures

Bibliography

Ashmore, N. & Moriarty, J. (2015) 'From student to artist: Supporting students' creative development through place-based work', *Journal of Writing in Creative Practice,* 8: 1, pp. 37–54

Barret, E. & Bolt, B. (2009) *Practice as Research: Approaches to Creative Arts Enquiry,* I.B. Taurus

Cecily Brown at Blenheim Palace, (2020-21) Blenheim Art Foundation, 17 September 2020 - 3 January 2021

Charney, D. (2011) *The Power of Making,* V&A

Dineen, R., Samuel, E. & Livesey, K. (2005) 'The Promotion of Creativity in Learners: Theory and Practice', *Art, Design and Communication in Higher Education,* (4) 3, pp.115-173

Hunt, C. (2000). *Therapeutic Dimensions of Autobiography in Creative Writing.* Jessica Kingsley Publishers

MacKinnon, D. W. (1970) 'Creativity: a multi-faceted phenomenon' in Roslansky, J. D. (ed) *Creativity: A Discussion at the Nobel Conference.* North-Holland Publishing Company

May, R. (1959) 'The nature of creativity', *ETC: A review of general semantics:* 261-276

Mooney, R. L. (1963) 'A conceptual model for integrating four approaches to the identification of creative talent' in Taylor, C.W. & Barron, F. (eds.) *Scientific Creativity: Its Recognition and Development,* John Wiley

Moriarty, J. (2017) 'Writing to Resist: Storying the Self and Audit Culture in Higher Education' in Cole, K. & Hassel, H. (eds.) *Surviving Sexism in Academia: Strategies for Feminist Leadership,* Routledge

Orsini-Jones, M. (2008) 'Troublesome language knowledge: Identifying threshold concepts in grammar learning' in *Threshold Concepts within the Disciplines.* Sense. pp. 213-226

Reading, C. & Moriarty, J. (2019) 'Walking and mapping our creative recovery' in Moriarty, J. (ed) *Autoethnographies from the Neoliberal Academy: Rewilding, writing and resistance,* Routledge

Tedlock, B. (2000) 'Ethnography and ethnographic representation' in Denzin, N. K. & Lincoln Y.S. (eds.), *Handbook of Qualitative Research,* Sage. p.468

You Can't Tell by Looking (2019). Tension Fine Art. Stuart Elliott, Julian Lowe and Mark Wallinger, curated by Kate Love. From 5 October 2019.

Inspiration and Play:

Enticing your creativity back into the open

The visual arts are not easy to uncover; in order to make them speak we need to question ourselves every time we question them. A complex art if ever there was one. There's a bit of everything in it, literature, observation, virtuosity (I won't say skill), gifts of the eye, music. More than anything the visual arts needs to be loved a great deal.
Paul Gauguin cited in Donatien Grau: 1951, p.16

Chris

I have just been to a seminar at the Tension Gallery in South London, a new space opened by Ken Turner, an old friend from Central St Martin's days. I go in part because I admire his commitment to this new venture and want to show support, but also because it's an opportunity to catch up with friends from 20 years ago and discover whether they are still making art. I am looking for a connection, a way back into my own art practice which has stalled, frozen. When I arrive, there is a group of about thirty people, some known faces, some new, all chatting in small groups. Feeling self-conscious, I look at the artwork and try to blend in, try and feel part of this event.

The exhibition and accompanying seminar, *You Can't Tell by Looking*, are curated by the artist, theorist and writer, Kate Love. On the walls of the gallery are works by three male painters of some repute, Stuart Elliot, Julian Lowe, and Mark Wallinger, alongside those of Kate. Kate was the critical art theory tutor when I was a student, and I was always in awe of her knowledge of, and commitment to, the arts. I knew she'd had cancer recently and was curious about the fact that her experiences did not seem to have stalled her creativity, that she was still writing and curating and talking about art. I found this inspiring and courageous given my own pitiful attempts to re-engage with my creativity (Kate died not long after the seminar. Her book, *An Affect of an Experience,* was published posthumously in 2020).

In the small gallery space Kate was chairing a discussion with all the exhibiting artists addressing the question of how you finish a painting – a conversation about the most important factors in finishing a painting, whether it is the marks the artist makes or what the painting represents? As I sat there amongst the small audience on the cold gallery floor, cross legged and uncomfortable, I realised I found the question ironic because what I wanted to ask her was, "How do you start a painting? How do you get going, keep going, given all that you have been through and continue to go through?" It is Kate I want to address this question to. I feel slightly hostile to the fact that the three artists on the panel are all male, but I stay silent and listen, intimidated by the weighty words they use and the highbrow concepts they toy with.

The discussion turns to the exhibiting artists' practice and processes, accounts of their long days in the studio, churning over ideas, fiddling with seemingly nonsensical things in the belief that something would eventually emerge, the importance of belief in one's own agency, even in the face of few tangible results or a lack of encouraging remarks from others, and how all of this takes bags of self-confidence and self-belief that what you are doing will lead to something. There are murmurs of agreement from the small audience. I wilt and feel a failure, knowing that I rarely spend more than an hour or so every few days engaged in any form of creative activity, let alone painting because the desire to be out in the world, walking the Downs or swimming in the sea, supersedes the urge to apply myself in a more focused way. Until this moment, I have justified this by telling myself that I need to prioritise these activities to stay well but now, listening to others at the seminar, I wonder if I am just letting myself off the hook. Do I need to apply myself? Turn up more?

Where has it been?

My creativity has been hibernating, buried deep beneath soft protective layers. Layers that consisted of occupying my time with comforting domestic tasks, gentle exercise, counselling, oodles of alternative therapy, weaponising organic food, and idling with a few trusted family members and select friends. Until now, I have been happy to let my creativity slumber, afraid that it will demand something from me, take me away from the activities that have supported me thus far, scared to rock the boat in case allowing creativity back into my life disturbs the strategies I rely on to get by, to feel well. And in truth I am fearful that if I remove the protective layers, I will find that my creativity has withered and died. As a child, in the 1960s I had a pet tortoise that I used to feed in front of the TV, fascinated by this strange little creature that crawled slowly but determinedly across the living room. As winter approached. my dad put it in a large box filled with soft straw, explaining that it needed to hibernate and that we would wake it up in the spring, but it never did wake up and instead we buried it in the back garden. So, it seemed to me that waking something up from a deep sleep is precarious. I am wary, there is no certainty.

Until now I have proceeded with caution, slowly engaging in a series of small creative activities at home, and now my house is littered with half completed projects. I plan to make chutney out of crops of apples from the garden but each time I go into the cold damp shed where they are stored, I simply register their disintegration as they turn from plump and green to brown and wrinkled and I turn away. Perhaps another year, I think to myself. Next to the chair where I sit in the evening, little squares of cut-up cloth from my son's old shirts sit in piles waiting to be turned into the quilt I planned to make him over a year ago. As if in protest, fed up with waiting, the squares mysteriously migrate to other places, finding other purposes for themselves – a rag to wipe the car windows, an impromptu hankie. Next to them are stacks of old photos destined to be added to family albums that have turned sticky with time and dust whilst I procrastinate. Each incomplete project a testament to my lack of confidence that it is safe to allow my creativity to surface, expand, thrive.

And whilst I do not paint, I do sometimes look over the work I have done in the past, examining it, considering it, wondering how I completed anything at all, amazed that I was capable of that. As time goes on, I visit occasional exhibitions, absorbing the work and marvelling at the commitment of other artists. In the evenings I sometimes sit looking at imagery from art history, drawing copies in a process that I find relaxing and meditative, but crucially not taxing or draining – and by working in this way, I feel like I am relearning a code that I was once more adept with.

I have taken heed of the experience of a friend whose husband was put into a medically-induced coma following a heart attack, a process that involved lowering his body temperature significantly to allow his body to heal – a forced period of hibernation that gave him the best chance of survival. It was waking him up, warming him slowly, that was the riskiest part of the procedure. In the end he recovered well, but somehow, I absorbed the message that something that is that cold or frozen needs to warm up very slowly.

After the seminar at the Tension Gallery, I begin to think I need a more productive focus to my creativity and challenge myself to do three things. Firstly, I decide to do a bit of housekeeping, tidying up my art room at home, which involves throwing away heaps of old work. I want to feel lighter and I give away paintings and prints to family and friends, considering that they are better in the world then stashed in my upstairs room. In the end, I am left with a clinically clean space with rows of sharpened pencils. It feels like something could start here.

Secondly, I decide to set aside painting for a while and try out some new activities that I think will be fun. I sign up to join a pottery class, working in a medium that is new to me. There is something about the feel of the clay, the connection to the earth that is appealing, and as I coil long lengths of slip to make my first pot, I enjoy the human contact that comes with being part of a class and delight in making something useful and practical. I remember a poem Jess wrote about me called Terracotta Woman and I wonder if somehow this poem has nudged me in the direction of clay? By the end of the course, I have made three rather clumsy-looking pots which I am delighted with and plan to give to my family for Christmas.

Terracotta Woman for Christina Reading

The clay is cooling
So she works fast.
Building the slip
From the floor up.
She moulds
The shoes
The skirt
The breasts.
Smoothing over defects
Suggesting imperfection,
Fissures in the terracotta
That would
Otherwise crack
This soldier
Before she's even done.
She drags her hands
Up the neck
Squeezing gently,
Giving definition
To space in the armour.
A spot where an adversary
Might learn to cut her down.
Elsewhere,
She makes the armour thick
And wide,
So warriors won't see the woman
Underneath.
Won't judge her
For a weakness
That isn't even there.

Thirdly, I am persuaded to sign up for the Brighton Art Fair by three artist friends, hopeful that this will encourage me to finally start painting again. I am excited and dare to think about what I might paint. Retrieving an old copy of Homer's *Iliad* whilst clearing my father-in-law's house after he died, I read this tale for the first time and find its narrative about the devastation brought about by war compelling. The book is illustrated with Flaxman's evocative designs, and I decide to use this to inspire a series of paintings, endeavouring to portray the experience of women, placing them centre stage rather than being an adjunct to the stories about the men. Pat Barker's novel, *The Silence of the Girls* (2018), does this in literary form and I read her novel to add to my understanding of the tale. What emerges from my efforts are images of women lamenting but supported by others and I decide that, although Jess and I agreed to make sculpture, it is these paintings that end up providing the apt metaphor for where my creativity has been, lost grieving, lamenting and where it is right now, tentative, hopeful, and needing support.

Figure 19: Women of the Iliad, No.1   *Figure 20: Women of the Iliad, No.4*

Task

Reflect on what being creative means to you.

- Write about your personal definitions of creativity
- Reflect on where your creativity is right now
- Make model/s of your creative self/selves

Share your thoughts, writing and artworks with a friend. What does the exercise and conversation with your friend show you about your creativity?

Try something new

Trying new things, being open to new experiences, can play a key role in helping to keep our motivation and interest in our own creativity alive (Beaty et al: 2016). In other words, there is a connection between our willingness to try new things and being creative. This exercise is about trying something new, having a go at something different and finding out what happens when you do that. That could be learning a new skill, trying a new material that you haven't used before, visiting a new place, or making a new friend. Be experimental. When we try new things, we venture into the unknown. You can't be sure what will happen, how you will feel or respond, or what will happen to the artwork you make or the writing you do. It's a risk. Take it. Notice how you feel, how you respond, and how you might draw upon these new experiences in your writing or artwork.

Figure 21: Women of the Iliad, No.8

The challenge is to make an artwork or write about something that is reflective of this new experience in any way that is personally meaningful to you.

Remaking the Patriarchy

Jess

I do not want to do this. Why have I agreed to make models of my creative selves? I tell my students to take risks and be brave, but my creativity is ordered. Known. I set deadlines I meet, I don't procrastinate, I write for hours if I need to and then cut and edit until it is ready to share. Success to me means outputs. Articles, chapters, edited books, books, conferences, seminars, workshops – tangible, listable things I can cross off my never-ending list. I am asked by colleagues *how do you do it?* and the answer is: I work hard, often late at night, I juggle family and career, I always feel guilty, I always feel I have more to give to the personal and the professional parts of my life. But of course, I never give this answer, instead I smile and bat the question away like it's nothing, like what I've achieved and what I have done is a trifle.

I seem to be aiming for something, getting somewhere, but I'm not sure where. I like to write and after all, how can I teach creative writing and not have empathy with my students about the insecurities, joys, challenges, and clarity that writing brings? I have written a lot: not all of it good. It is the job and some days I feel untouchable and the writing flows or the editing is instinctive and some days I feel like I am regurgitating, pushing, toiling and when I read it back, it still jars. But even then, I have confidence that sharing it for critique with my community of writers will give me ideas to shift and refresh that mean I will get it done. Get it done. That is where my creativity is at. Get. It. Done.

I do not have time to make models. My inner censor (Antoniou, 2004) is already laughing, already wondering what I think I'm doing. I can't even draw stick people! This will just be a mess. I leave it over a week. Buy the materials in advance and leave them on the sideboard, let them stare at me. Feel guilty about it. *Get. It. Done.*

Finally, I take out the plasticine, make the time to try. I roll the navy clay between my hands.

What to do?

It is unyielding at first, and won't give in. The warmth of my skin feeds it, the clay taking on the lines in my hand, the shape of my palm. I wish it wasn't blue. So male. Conservative. I knead, shaping the patriarchy this child's toy has come to mean, wanting to create something perfect, beautiful, impressive. But I lack the skill and that scares me. The not knowing is uncomfortable. There is no ecstasy or drive to do this. All I can make is sausages, long and thin. Unsolid. What can I make with a sad sausage?

And then I see it.

A little man with a little hat and small penis. Spindly legs and arms imploring, wanting more. His eyes are deep set and his mouth discontented and hard to please. I know this man! He is the conventional academic voice. Peer reviewer, interview panel, funding judge. Finding fault, looking for the worst.

Figure 22. My creativity (Jess) No.1

Audience – male, traditional, conventional, not easily pleased, joyless.

Figure 23: My creativity (Jess) No.2

Creative self – wielding her pen. Fulfilled, resting at present but not inactive, waiting.

Adam needs his Eve: my creative self. She is easy to build, her shape familiar and pleasurable. Making her brings me joy. I mould the breasts and hips and give her a pencil. She wants to rest, to sit, but her arms are ready to work. She is smiling. Is this because she is happy or is the smile fixed in place to please people? I'm not sure.

Figure 24: My creativity (Jess) No.3

Creative process – locked up in a neat ordered box. Needs opening, interaction, play, risk.

My creative process needs form, it is not human. It is hiding, but from what or whom? I place them in a tableau. Playing with each figure, making up stories, no longer worried about perfection or style. This is what it is; where I am at:

Figure 25: My creativity (Jess) No.4

67

My creative self, resting in the forest. She is outside in the light. Her audience is waiting in a corner, ready to judge and critique. My creative self needs to find the key and unlock her box of creativity so she can move past her current audience and walk towards new adventures.

I get it done. But I am brighter. Lighter. Different. This is new.

List of Figures

Bibliography

Antoniou, M. (2004) 'My Cypriot Cookbook: Re-imagining My Ethnicity', *Auto/Biography*, 12(2):126

Barker, P. (2018) *The Silence of the Girls*, Penguin

Beaty, Roger E., et al. 'Creative cognition and brain network dynamics'. *Trends in Cognitive Sciences* 20.2 (2016): 87-95

Grau, D. (2016) *Ramblings of a Wannabe Painter, Paul Gauguin*, David Zimmer

I am a Wanderer (2018) Modern Art Oxford Exhibition, Kiki Smith, 28 October 2019 - 19 January 2020

Pope, A. (1878) *The Iliad of Homer* (Translation). George Bell & Sons

You Can't Tell by Looking (2019) Tension Fine Art. Stuart Elliott, Julian Lowe and Mark Wallinger, curated by Kate Love. From 5 October 2019

Chapter 3: New Intentions

Walk 3: Chanctonbury Ring – The Return

Walking and talking humanise my life, draw it to an ancient and comforting scale. We live as we move, a step at a time, and there is something in gentle walking that reminds me how I must live.

(Cameron: 2002, p.1)

This chapter interweaves Chris and Jess's voices. Jess's narrative is in italics to distinguish between them.

We are not getting this wrong. Not today.

I have different shoes – wellingtons, but the fancy kind that my mum donated to me after a wardrobe cull. They are the most expensive shoes I own. As we trek up the slope to the South Downs, I am surer of foot than before; I don't sporadically stumble or swear. Even in the torrential rain and amidst rivulets of gunge, I feel ready. My additional January ballast means I warm up after the first bend. I'm not as fit as the last time we did this but I'm unusually unfazed by the extra pounds. It is now four years since I had a melanoma removed and for the first time in ages, Christmas was decadent and relaxing instead of tied up with fear and uncertainty. It was worth it, indulgence without the fear and guilt that I am giving myself cancer, without the nagging thought that it is all my fault and better to punish myself and abstain, abstain. When we reach the top, my breathing levels and I feel relieved when the pathway evens out and the hard incline stops.

Chris reminds me that we were here two years ago, not one as I had imagined. Time slips. It has been ten years since we spoke at a symposium in Berlin and I almost missed my son's first birthday when our flight was cancelled. Since then, I have organised conferences in Brighton or ventured as far as Bristol, so I don't have to travel far from home. We both wonder where that decade has gone. Part of it in recovery, part of it finishing our theses, part watching our children grow and, in Chris's case, seeing them leave the family home, and in mine, finishing college and junior school. We have also written two chapters for a book on autoethnography (Moriarty & Reading, 2019) where we committed to walk and write and even change. On our first walk at Chanctonbury Ring, we got lost and had to turn back. We both felt frustrated and thwarted but justified losing our way as a necessary part of the creative process. I am not here today to get lost. We are here to find a way.

Figure 26: Wellington Boots - Chanctonbury Ring Revisited

A good night's sleep goes a long way; I wake up early, excited about the walk despite the grey clouds and the foreboding forecasts on the radio about unprecedented wind – Hurricane Brendan apparently. I eat porridge, pack sandwiches, blister plasters and water into my rucksack. I am prepared. I even take a photo of the OS section of the map covering the area we will walk. This walk is unfinished business, a returning to and a reclaiming of a route we failed to complete almost two years ago. There is a touch of anxiety associated with my determination to close the circuit that has been left open like a door ajar in my mind all this time. It seems important to my sense of recovery to get it right this time, proof I have moved on, a sign of hope.

Figure 27: The Chalk Path, Chanctonbury Ring Revisited

I start off in the direction I believe we took the last time but Chris states, kindly but firmly, that this is rubbish. No wonder we got lost. My interior GPS has never worked. Maybe that's another reason why I struggle to leave places? I have lived most of my life in Brighton and worked at the university for twenty years. Creativity needs risk and adventure; it values getting lost and mapping new paths. I don't. I follow Chris into the mist, but she is more apprehensive today. She will be 60 this year and we talk about her walking party and family holiday to Greece. She speaks about it like it is an inevitable rather than joyful thing on the horizon, but I try and persuade her it can be both.

Figure 28: Jess in the rain, Chanctonbury Ring Revisited

We decide to walk the route back to front. Rather than heading straight to the Ring, we opt instead to start where we would have ended, an unknown chalky track that runs south towards the sea. There are of course no rules to say which is the start and which is the finish, but habits are hard to break. Walking in the direction of the Ring would have felt familiar, usual, after years of bringing children and dogs up here, and it's hard to walk in a different direction and call it the start, but we do. Heading off, I am already drenched, so is Jess. Neither of us mentions turning back. Not to complete the walk this time is unthinkable. And I reflect that this is the third walk we have done for this project on creative recovery – all so far have been in the company of howling gales and icy rain, the weather doing all it can to deter us from venturing out, venturing on.

I speak of needing change. Paul and I have been talking about moving back to Brighton city centre or to outside of Galway. At long last I have applied for an Irish passport and the misery of a looming Brexit and five years of a Tory government seem unbearable. I have lived in the suburbs of Brighton almost all my life and I feel grateful but also stuck. Finding a way out on this walk is inextricably tied up with escape elsewhere and I am utterly focused on getting there. Chris is encouraging and we walk and dream about a wellness centre and new starts. The terrain is known and not scary. Even when we aren't sure, we seem to be going forward.

Figure 29: Sheep in the rain, Chanctonbury Ring revisited

The wind eases and Jess talks about a possible move to Ireland, dreams of setting up a retreat centre in rural Galway, the seat of her ancestors, buoyed up by the promise of her new Irish passport. What a fabulous plan. Butting up against this is the reality of her everyday life, her children's lives in Saltdean where they now live, and her work. It's an idea that needs form, legs. It's so hard to change your life, I reflect, and we are all wedded to our routines, our habits, our localities, to our networks of friends and family that fill and give meaning to our daily lives. Real change is challenging, an assault on all that is familiar, disruptive for all involved, so unless we are pushed, we hover on the precipice, admiring the view, imagining what we would do in these other lives that we don't lead. It would take a leap of faith, a jump into the unknown and Jess has a lot to lose: friends, a job and family. Her bones are in Sussex. But I take from this conversation her desire for adventure, for something new, boredom perhaps with the familiar. But it is encouraging that she has the space to imagine and dream this other life and there is a freedom and a sign of recovery of sorts in that. A retreat centre in Saltdean, I say flippantly. She laughs but is not impressed. She has plans to go to Ireland at half term.

Figure 30: Horse field, Chanctonbury Ring revisited

I notice Chris taking photos of me in secret, but I try not to go berserk, hoping she will draw again. Last time we did this walk, she had stopped painting after cancer and now she has started again. I will her on and away from that dark place when we were lost and scrabbling around for a pathway out. We enter a field with the biggest horse I have ever seen, and I talk to him jovially to try and ease Chris's fear. Two more horses hover at the gate and Chris all but canters across the field to escape. The horses don't care though, showing only mild interest as we make our way.

I listen to Jess talk about her plans for the coming years, books to edit, a sabbatical, a professorship, funding bids. I try to think of something interesting to say about what I am doing, what I am proposing. It sounds minuscule and inconsequential, self-indulgent and laughable in comparison, another universe. I am taking music lessons, I say. The recorder is something I learnt as a child and I am picking up where I left it 50 years ago. Despite my family's mirth at my squeaky practice sessions, I revel in deciphering the musical notes on the page. When I tell her what I am doing Jess squirms, recounting her own school-day memories of playing this unforgiving instrument. But I am going back to re-engage with music in the only way I know how. What an idiot I feel. But there it is, this is what I am doing.

The weather is so dreadful that we don't stop for lunch; instead we share biscuits and stride on. Last time, we looked for points in the distance we could map our journey by, we asked our phones and men in Lycra for help and still got lost. Today, everything is familiar and the route seems easy. We are practically bounding up the hill, watched by sheep and cows who look peeved by the storm. Suddenly the ring appears out of the mist, out of nothing, just as it did the first time. The black trees beautiful against the fog and sky, connected by branch and root in a circle, like a gathering at a party we haven't been invited to but are happy to watch.

Figure 31: Chanctonbury Ring revisited

There it is before us, the place where we turned round on our last walk. Jess recognises it immediately.

"There's the vineyard where we got lost last time!" she yells excitedly.

I am slower to allow the familiarity to sink in, that sense of *déjà vu*. Even though we are soaked to the skin and cold, very cold, we are relaxed, we are making good progress. We are doing what we set out to do and a building sense of euphoria accompanies us. First sheep and then Chanctonbury Ring emerge out of the mist.

I am pleased with the morning's work. I think I can say I have achieved something by completing this walk. I have reassessed my relationship to this terrain, closed the loop and the sense of failure that has bugged me since the first time we attempted it. Two and a half hours, eleven and a half kilometres. I had expected it to be more arduous, to take longer. I wonder why the first effort to walk this route was so arduous and fraught. This time round the walk is in the bones, the GPS internal. Completing the walk seems important because it's a moment to reassess the past and the route we have travelled to get here, professionally, creatively, and personally, since our first effort. Somehow it frees us to plan, to look to the future.

We make it back to the car in record time.
"How did it take us so long before?" Chris wonders, and we trace our steps and reflect on what might change.

"We were lost?" I offer when the sums don't add up and we still can't find the two hours we seem to have made up.

In the car on the way home, we shiver as the water and cold seep into our bones. We turn the radiator way up high and plan our next steps. I tell Chris I am going to rewrite a myth and she promises to draw. Today it seems effortless. But strangely it seems as if we both almost miss the struggle. Maybe because that's what we have known for so long now. Maybe because creativity needs challenge and change. Maybe because we are women who can't bring ourselves to enjoy the moments when everything just works. But maybe these are the kind of women we can be now, post-cancer, and maybe this book will help us to accept those women and come to know them and love them once more.

List of Figures

Bibliography

Cameron, J. (2002) *Walking in this World: Practical Strategies for Creativity,* Random House

Moriarty, J. & Reading, C. (2019) 'Walking and Mapping Our Creative Recovery: an interdisciplinary method' in Moriarty, J. (ed) *The Neoliberal Academic: An autoethnographic rewilding,* Routledge

Using your personal archives to reconnect with your creativity

I reflected that my creativity could be traced back to my early years, cultural background and the influences that have shaped my life. Not least, my heritage and childhood.

(Evaristo: 2021, p.37)

Chris

At the time of writing, I am three years on from my operation to remove my tumour. I have learnt to live with the ebbs and flows of my terror and look forward to moving on from the stuck place that cancer instigated, to search for ways to support my creative recovery, to reinvigorate my love of painting, to find out what else I want to do now... next. The research that Jess and I have done tells me to go back and recount my autobiographical experiences to help me make sense of my journey to be an artist and frame future decisions with the knowledge of this scaffold behind me (Reading & Moriarty, 2010). So, I set out to practise what I preach, to find out if telling my own story can help me set a new course, or at least provide clues and insights into my creative process and where I want to take it next. What emerges is a story, my story of how I became an artist, a reflection and reassessment of my personal, professional and creative life so far. This has not been a straightforward road, it has been full of twists and turns, dead-ends and U-turns but reflecting on these experiences will, I believe, help me pave the way for future creative endeavours.

'Remember me Chris'

My abiding memory of my grandmother is that to celebrate my first Holy Communion, when I was about 4 years old, my grandmother gave me a prayer book inscribed with the words 'Remember me Chris'. She died, aged 86, in 1992 – nearly twenty years ago – and now when I read those words scrawled across the page, I wonder now how I have honoured that appeal.

My grandmother was always buying and selling second-hand clothes at Paddy's Market in Liverpool. In the morning she would tie her large money bag around her middle and head out to work with what she referred to as 'the stuff'. 'The stuff' mainly consisted of second-hand clothes but her hoards were also known to include gold, silver and antiques. On her business card was the description of her trade: *Buyer and Seller of Quality Used Clothes*. A generation before, her father had also been in the second-hand clothes business, a wardrobe dealer according to census returns, buying and selling clothes from small premises in Shore Street, Liverpool. So, clothes were the family business: they were in the blood. And, as a family, it's fair to say that we loved hunting for clothes, old and new.

A stroke at the age of 40 had left my grandmother with a lopsided gait, an arm with no feeling hanging down one side of her body and a slow heaviness in the way she walked. Her uneven bearing defined her way of being, of doing everything one-handed: cooking, sewing, and smoking Woodbines. My mother recounts how setting out in a taxi on a Monday morning, my grandmother would make her way across town from Anfield, a place of small, terraced houses with lavatories in the back yard, to leafier parts of town, such as Sefton Park, where she would leave her card and letter of introduction on the doormats of the well-to-do. Over the week, she would wait as small envelopes landed on the matt inviting her to call to view the 'stuff' at an appointed time and then she would head back, hat on, making her calls from house to house, bulk-buying the cast-offs, buying 'the stuff'. And I recall my mother's memories too, how as children, my mother and her three siblings were left in a nearby café whilst granny made her calls. She would return not just with bundles of clothes, but with stories provided by glimpses into these other women's lives.

"She lives on nuts and yogurt for tea!" my grandmother exclaimed after a visit to one wealthy client, a vegetarian.

This was how business was done in the days before phones, slowly, courteously every bit as efficiently. She traded these wares at Paddy's market on a Saturday morning (reputedly alongside Cilla Black's mum). Whenever we visited, making the pilgrimage up the M5 from our Gloucestershire village, this is where we would find her, not at home making dinner or cakes but out at work. In between sale days, these rails and bags of clothes were sorted and stored in the front parlour of her terraced house. Tightly packed musty furs sat alongside old ball-gowns or well-worn tweeds. Rummaging through them was like standing on the edge of a dense forest of heavy hanging garments, the act of pushing them apart forming passageways into other mysterious worlds. My mum and her sisters would appraise the latest hauls according to the quality of the cloth. Silk, cotton and wool were prized, alongside designer names that have long since faded. As a child, I watched them try things on and chat animatedly about what fitted, what suited, what items my grandmother might let them keep – they were, after all, her livelihood.

Clothes seemed a bonding thing. Even now, the first thing I look at when buying clothes is what they are made of, the quality of the cloth. I don't remember coveting any of these clothes for myself, my tastes were shaped by the 1970s' glam rock era of my teenage years: by glitter, platform soles and furry jackets. But when I was 18 years old and just about to head off to Brighton Polytechnic, my grandmother gave me a red fur squirrel coat. Not PC of course but I loved it and wore it constantly.

I don't remember Granny as glamorous. Most days she wore big heavy clothes and black, manly shoes suitable for cold days on the market store. Her large feet, an enormous size 11, were inherited by my mother, who would forever live with the accusation of elephantiasis and an impossible search for shoes. Shopping for shoes was a backdrop to my childhood and I counted myself lucky to be let off with a size 9.5. Still freakishly large, but it was just about possible to squeeze my feet into a pair of high street shoes.

Figure 32: Clothes rail

Granny came from a large, spirited Irish Catholic family that had settled in Liverpool the generation before. She was a woman who worked hard for a living and from this I took the importance of a woman's working life, the presumption of it. Education too was valued and although she had little formal schooling herself, she was proud that she had cousins who went to Dublin University and who she referred to as 'scholars' or 'learned'. But my grandmother's talents lay not only in making money but also in her practical talent for sewing clothes for her children, and although I have no memories of her sewing, the hum of her old treadmill Singer sewing machine, which was used constantly by my mother, provided another part of my childhood soundtrack.

What did all this have to do with being an artist? Nothing, I thought, until decades later, as a mature art student in my 30s at Central St Martin's, these rails of second-hand clothes turned up in my artworks, forming the subject of photographs, prints and paintings throughout the five years I studied there. I traipsed around the second-hand clothes shops of Brighton, buying things that interested me, dresses and shoes mainly, or rummaging through my own back catalogue of items hidden away in cupboards at home. I was attracted to the sense of history and faded glamour found in these racks of second-hand items and to the slightly musty smell that accompanied them that made me think of my grandmother's parlour. My playful explorations with these items took many different forms, installations made of clothes or photographic negatives pin-pricked or sewn together. Looking back now, I think what was passed down to me from my grandmother was a sense that clothing was important to a woman's story, whether those were clothes she made herself or clothes she bought and wore, and that second-hand clothes told stories of wear and tear, of degeneration and change but also of second chances and renewal. They were metaphors for the lives of the women who wore them. Clothes, I discovered, were the place where social history and personal histories collided in the most intimate and powerful way, providing me with a constant source of inspiration for my artworks.

Figure 33: The Mothers, No 5 out of 8

More recently, when I thought I had left this subject matter behind, an aunt from Australia whom I had not seen for twenty years said, "That looks like my mother" in response to a series of paintings called *The Mothers* (2012) which I had produced during my doctoral work as a representation of melancholy within the art history of women's figurative art. Seemingly (in terms of subject matter) *The Mothers* had nothing to do with my grandmother but my aunt's comment made me realise that these were paintings of women in the era when my grandmother would have been a young woman. I was using imagery from archive film (The Southern Railway Servants Orphange at Woking (c. 1926) Screen Archives South East) as source material for my paintings, attempting to convey some sense of the women's lives in the film. But looking at the paintings again, I realised that in the portrayal of these women, the heavy clothes, and their cheerful demeanour in the face of hardship, I had not only addressed the lives of the unknown women in the film but also aspects of my grandmother's life, or at least a sense of her. Looking back at these paintings now I can see an echo of the clothes my grandmother and my aunts wore, the female camaraderie and the rhythm of her slow burdensome walk which I witnessed as a child.

This realisation matters because my doctoral work turned out to be about my grandmother in part. In a sense, the connections with my grandmother's life were vague and distant, yet a certain obsession in my artwork with clothing and posture, interpreted through the lens of the history of women's figurative art, bears witness to my memories of the slow, heavy yet determined way she walked and the way she dressed. I like to imagine an affinity between my grandmother, myself and the women in my paintings, a conversation about work and children and the personal challenges faced by each of us despite the distance of time. In other words, I was working with some sense of this fusion between personal story and social history as it was revealed through women's experience of their body and the clothing they wore, and this was prompted (in part I am sure) by my early memories of my grandmother and her racks of clothes.

Looking back through old black and white photographs of Mum and Dad, they look young and glamorous. They were just 19 and 21 years old respectively when they met, so when I arrived 9 months later, they were still just figuring life out. Dad engaged in endless DIY projects, redecorating the homes I lived in with my mum and younger sister, Louise (another sister, Laura, arrived later). The smell of burnt paint unleashed by the Bunsen burner as he scraped off the fumy old paint from doors, the turps he used to clean his brushes, are smells I remember from childhood. I think perhaps my affinity with painting started here. After the weeks of careful preparation came the moment of painting. Clean sweeps of fresh white paint transformed the house, making it our own. I was often called upon to lend a hand and developed a familiarity with the tools of painting: the brushes, rags, and turps. Big brushes for the ceiling and walls, medium brushes for doors, and tiny, neat brushes for the edges of the windows panes. For a while Dad was a self-employed decorator and I would earn pocket money by helping, climbing rickety ladders and painting ceilings. I think these early experiences of house decorating made me understand that painting offered a sense of renewal, as previously run-down spaces were charged with new possibilities, new histories waiting to be written on those walls. It was a functional activity that engaged the whole body rather than something that was necessarily cerebral or indulgent, and that need to work with big brushes and clean sweeps of paint still drives much of my approach to painting today. When Dad was not doing up houses, he would be out in the garden, making bird boxes, building bonfires, growing beans. Always making, always doing.

Mum worked at the local gas board as a clerk, cycling back at the end of the day to make curtains, clothes, cushions and pots of jam, in a constant creative domestic flow. An annual batch of plum jam was always burnt but we became accustomed to the taste of that sticky preserve with a supply that lasted most of the year. Like my grandmother, Mum liked to sew, and I remember her sitting at an old Singer sewing machine, her foot rocking back and forth, making dresses, coats and trousers for my sister and me. I wore these clothes throughout my childhood and looked forward to Mum's new creations until one day, just after I had just started secondary school, I was in town wearing a new dress – a flamboyant gingham in the style of Dorothy from the Wizard of Oz – when I encountered the cool kids from school in their trendy shop-bought clothes. Instead of pride in my attire, I felt instantly embarrassed. The next week, aged 13, I got a Saturday job at Woolworth and quickly discovered Chelsea Girl (a high street chain popular with teenagers at the time) where I would buy pencil skirts and acrylic jumpers to fit in with my school friends. My aspirations at the time were governed by what I could buy from that store with my meagre earnings.

Figure 34. Dad as a young boy

I took from Mum and Dad in their different ways the importance of fashioning your own life, shaping your day with doing, with making, whether that was jam, painting windows, or making dresses. Things didn't need to be the best or the most beautiful but being able to say "I did that" mattered, that you had put something of yourself into whatever you made, an understanding that however beautiful or lovely something you bought was, the satisfaction of making a thing for yourself was prized more or differently.

Dad was born in 1938, reputedly the unclaimed son of an unknown American, leaving my other grandmother, Elfreda, a single mother – not an easy option back then. Although he never talked about it, choosing instead to focus on raising his own family, I nevertheless picked up a sense of sadness from him. Recently my husband, John, has become interested in tracing his ancestry and investigated my dad's family, tracing a link back through the maternal line to the Knights Templar in the 13th century. Dad would have liked that, filling a hole in the understanding of where he has come from, however distant.

Alongside other things Dad had tried – butchering in an abattoir (a most unsuitable occupation for a man of his sensitive disposition), shovelling coal on the railways, doing National Service in the RAF, and working in an engineering company – he also talked about himself as a pilot in a war he was too young to have fought in, a life-saving brain surgeon, and an as-yet-undiscovered artist on a par with Picasso. Dad joked that his absent father was the American movie star, John Wayne. There was something in the manner of this movie star that resonated with Dad, the quiet hero, the lonesome cowboy, which meant that whenever this actor appeared in our home via the TV, Dad seemed to go into a sort of reverie, watching the actor for signs of himself.

After we moved from our council flat opposite the secretive warrens of the Government Communications Head Quarters (or GCHQ as it is more commonly known) to a suburban semi in the village of Church Down, Dad's brother jokingly referred to him as 'The Squire'. Certainly, he dressed the part, choosing a gentleman's outfit of fine tweeds and brown brogues bought at Cheltenham's best tailor's shop, *The Famous,* using clothing to imbue the qualities of class that he aspired to. I learnt that clothes signified how you wanted to be seen. He played with these alternative versions of himself, telling tales that were exaggerated truths, so that real and make-believe blur in my recollections of him. When I remember Dad, I remember the man he was and the life he led, but also the lives he didn't lead – the ones he alluded to in his fabricated tales.

In her paper on the 'Therapeutic Effects of Writing Fictional Autobiography' (2010), Celia Hunt reports on her ongoing research into the relationship between the fictionalising process and an understanding of the self. Hunt writes that:

> ...*fictional autobiography often leads to increased reflexivity of self. I am beginning to understand this psychic movement as an emotional and conceptual shift towards a more fluid and flexible self-experience, involving the development of mental agency grounded first and foremost in the physically and emotionally felt body rather than in self-concept. It is a felt expansion in sense of self, which brings with it an increased ability to act and think*

(Hunt: 2010, p. 232)

Hunt argues that this process "involved a move away from a sense of fixity or 'stuckness' in one or more dominant self-concepts, an increased awareness of spontaneous bodily feelings and emotions and a more reflective relationship" (ibid, p.232).

With hindsight, I think this tendency for narrative, for fictionalising, for storytelling, was crucial to my father – an instinctive way of moving away from a fixed sense of himself and embracing other aspects of himself through a reflective, imaginative process. This storytelling trait had the advantage of making the world of the imagination a real thing in my life. Somehow this tendency to fictionalise his experience brought us closer together because his way of being, which existed between the real and the imagined lives he led, allowed me a certain scope, a certain freedom; I was not to be defined solely by the material facts of my existence. What I dreamt about and imagined mattered too.

I believe too that this fictionalising process deployed by my father was pivotal to my own development as an artist because it showed me how to inhabit the space of the imaginary, to give myself permission to play with ideas and carry the idea of being an artist with me until the time I allowed myself to make artwork. It enabled me to understand, at a personal level, the value of the imaginary as a place of empathy, humour, hope and aspiration, set against the everyday practical challenges of my life.

Even as a child I understood that my mum was glamorous. She had thick black hair, soft hazel green eyes and a wide, usually lipsticked smile. Her style echoed the 1950s movie stars Bette Davis and Sophia Loren, rather than the swinging sixties. Mum had grown up in Liverpool, the daughter of an Irish

Catholic market trader and an Irish Protestant grocer. As a city girl, Mum's dress was a bit sharper than the county look that prevailed in the Gloucestershire village where she moved to when she married Dad and where I grew up. Instead of BHS and M&S, Mum tended to wear either clothes she had made, or the 'posh' second-hand clothes given to her by her mother.

It is perhaps no surprise that the shared and individual experiences of my grandmother, mother and me found their way into my artworks. Painful sculptures of shoes with pins inside, wax sculptures of feet tottering precariously on thin heels, paintings of oversized shoes, or shoes as dreams or unreachable things in the stars. Mountains of shoes jumbled together, or in neat inert rows. There was a fascination with the normality of these everyday items which posed such a challenge to many of the women in my family. Looking back, I think I was emphasising the physical and emotional pain of these moments that were unspoken and tolerated at the time. As a teenager walking back from clubs late at night, I would often go barefoot, unable to cope with the blisters and pain caused by ill-fitting shoes. Over the years I have reached a sort of accommodation with my feet, buying Birkenstocks for the summer and a pair of sturdy expensive Danish boots in the winter. This footwear is not exciting but serviceable, allowing me to walk without pain, and yet I still find that my paintings include the motif of women with large feet shod in heavy footwear and this I think goes back still to memories of my grandmother.

Storytelling and creativity

I tell these stories about the impact of memories and autobiographical experiences on my creative processes during my arts education to remind myself that my creativity comes from me and all that is, or has been, part of my life, and that my creativity thrives when I make work that engages with these past or present experiences, whether I chose to draw, paint, write or experiment with a new medium.

Telling tales about my grandmother reminds me that I can tap into the treasure trove of my personal archive of memories and experiences at any time and use them to inspire and motivate me. This provides me with a constant flow of sources of inspiration and enables me to make work that is personal and meaningful to me. Returning to these memories of my grandmother and my family allows me to rekindle their part in my autobiographical story, renewing my sense of connection to them and enabling me to see these experiences in a new way, through the lens of the stories I tell and the artwork I make. Hence, I find that half-remembered memories and fragments of stories are retrieved and granted a new significance by retelling these stories.

Moreover, I find that representing and reflecting on these experiences through the artworks I make and the stories I tell helps me to gain confidence and strengthens my personal voice in relation to my creative sense of self, helping me to know myself a little better and understand my inheritance and the connections between my past and my present.

The power of accessing your personal archives is that the stories they inspire are individual and unique to you. In this sense, I see this process not just as a creative act but also a feminist one, as it places the specific nature of my lived experience and memories at the centre of my creative process and each story or artistic endeavour by women adds to the diversity of representations of our experiences, mirroring women's lives in more detailed and accurate ways, and strengthening our symbolic world.

> *Awakening cultural memory isn't all retrospection or*
> *nostalgia; the process sets in play active re-inscriptions,*
> *laying the emphasis on the visionary potential of seeing*
> *something afresh.*
>
> (Warner: 2018, p.175)

So, what does looking back in this way enable me to do in the present? In Marina Warner's study of *Dreaming the Territory* (2017), an artwork by the landscape artist Jumana Emil Abboud, she describes how the artist's quest is to map memories of lost stories associated with 'special' places (special because a saint's relics for instance might be buried there) with multi-layered artworks that consist of layers of drawing, watercolour and film. Warner sees Abboud's approach to her artwork as involving "telling a different, fresh story about past relations between people and places, and strengthening them in the present" (ibid, p.175). Her remarks highlight once again the significance of mining the past for the present day. I would argue that comes from making visible all that has gone before and allowing us to see new experiences as related to, and building on, these histories. In this sense, accessing your personal archives not only acts as a power tool to rejuvenate your creativity by providing unique source material for stories and artworks, but also allows us to see the connections between all that has gone before and our creativity in the present day.

Going forward, I focus on what matters to me most right now, post-illness, and decide to embark on a series of small sketches and paintings of my family sourced from the pile of photographs of family gatherings from the distant and recent past littering the house. I use these images as starting points to try to find a way back into painting, to reconnect with my creativity in a meaningful way. It turns out to be a contemplative process with time spent looking and looking, drawing and redrawing, an image of somebody I love, who mattered to me. I found this motivated me. In the small series of paintings I made, what I saw reflected back was not just a likeness of my daughter, son, mother, sister, husband but a merger between my memories of the person and my imaginative interpretation of the image of them. But certainly, I can say that tapping into this store of auto-biographical memories and allowing myself to focus on what matters to me right now has motivated me to move away from my stuck place.

Figure 35: My daughter Lizzie

Task

Processes of reflecting on, and reviewing, your autobiographical experiences are important because they can bring your interests and motivations more fully into view and enable you to draw on these experiences in your creative work. In this chapter, I describe how I wrote stories and made artworks inspired by my own autobiographical stories and, in doing so, I found that the process improved confidence and self-belief in my creative sense of self by allowing me to see these memories as a personal archive that I can draw upon to connect with and inspire my creativity, and enabling me to see all that I have experienced so far as providing context for my creativity now and in future.

- Who has been influential in your creativity in your past?
- Make artwork or write a story in relation to an autobiographical memory (real or imagined) of a person who is important to you and your creativity.
- Describe them. What can you recall in terms of gestures, shapes, colour or other characteristics?
- Do you have a specific memory of that person that has inspired your creativity? Think about this memory in terms of all the senses of sight, hearing and touch.
- How is this memory related to your creativity now and in the future?
- Share your reflections with a creative friend. What do you learn about your creative sense of self?

List of Figures

Figure 32. Clothes rail (2001). Oil on Canvas. 150cm X 120cm.
Figure 33. The Mothers, No 5 out of 8 (2015). Oil on Aluminium. 18cm x 24cm.
Figure 34. Dad as a young boy (2012). Oil on Canvas. 60cm x 50cm.
Figure 35. My daughter Lizzie (2012). Oil on Canvas. 60cm x 50cm.

Bibliography

Evaristo, B. (2021). 'The Shape of Me', *The Guardian*, 25 September 2021. https://bit.ly/creativeN

Hunt, C. (2010). 'Therapeutic effects of Writing Fictional Autobiography', *Life Writing*, 7:3 231-244

Reading, C. (2009). 'Sources of Inspiration: How design students learn from museum and archive collections,' *Art, Design and Communication in Higher Education*, 8(2) pp.109-121

Reading, C. & Moriarty, J. (2010). 'Creative Partnerships: helping creative writing and visual practice students to make links between their creative processes and their personal, vocational and academic development', *Journal of Creative Writing in Creative Practice*, 3 (3) pp 285- 298)

Warner, M. (2018) *Forms of Enchantment. Writings on Art and Artists.* Thames and Hudson

Chapter 4: Embracing Uncertainty

Walk 4: Balcombe Circular via Ardingly Reservoir

Figure 36: Balcombe Circular No 6

This chapter interweaves Chris and Jess's voices. Jess's narrative is in italics to distinguish between them.

Before we set off, we decide that the focus of this walk will be our willingness to let go of the versions of ourselves and our creativity identified by our experiences of cancer, and to open ourselves to new versions and possibilities.

When Chris pulls out the three pages of instructions, my instinct is to snatch them out of her hand and rip them into tiny pieces. We are grown women writing a book on being creative! We don't need instructions. We can risk getting lost and find a way back.

The detail of the instructions feels necessary to guide our way, but irksome too because stopping to check the directions every few yards slows our pace and interrupts the normally reassuring steady rhythm of our walking. Holding the map means that my gloveless hands quickly feel numb on this frosty morning.

"It's like following a recipe though, isn't it?"

"What do you mean?" Chris asks, folding the instructions away and pointing in the direction of a boggy field.

"Well, anyone can follow a recipe, can't they? What's special about that? Surely it's the finding your own way that is creative?"

Chris disagrees.

"But when we learn something new, we all need some instruction, no?"

I think back to learning to write, tracing my name and then copying it exactly. I think of the instruction I give my students to help them tell stories and checklists I suggest they use for assessments. I think of learning to hula hoop last year and the instructor's invaluable guidance and how much fun I had learning something new in this way, something I had feared suddenly giving me joy. A child's game pushing and challenging me, making me sweat and shout and laugh.

"Alright, where now?" I ask less begrudgingly.

Everything is frosty. Winter is here and it's early enough that the sun still hasn't touched the footpaths and country stiles. Everything is precarious and, in my trainers, I slip and slide and swear. Chris is in her sturdy walking boots and waterproof trousers, happy to crack the ice on muddy pebbles and venture through thick mud. We are ankle deep and my feet are already sodden when we hit the first marker and admire the sun rising behind a cornfield and the woodland beyond. I have to focus on not falling while Chris talks about the book and what we need to do. I see a structure forming and imagine the pages we will write. It feels tangible and real, like this walk. We planned to do it and now here we are, one foot in front of the slimy other, making our way, feeling certain we will finish.

A man in the sort of truck landowners have – they are always called Trojan or Warrior or something and seem to me to be some sort of compensation for an insecurity but are probably just useful in the mud – stops to tell us we should be walking on the same side of the road.

"You're right." I give a clenched smile, but he doesn't notice and continues to tell me about road safety in a very jolly voice. Chris is smirking from the other side of the road as I try not to roll my eyes.

"Thank you so much!" I give him a full beam as I wave him off and then rant for the following twenty minutes about not wanting to be told what to do by a man.

Figure 37: Balcombe Circular No 2

The following day I set pen to paper, a delayed response to the walk, already a memory of a walk. I feel laggardly, not sure what I want to say, undecided what to focus on. I could dwell on the clear crisp bright blue sky with a fierce, eye-blinding, white sun that lay low in the morning sky, so welcome after weeks of grey skies and persistent rain, the grassy fields that had a soggy depth, making colanders of Jess's city trainers, the endless stiles that offered respite from the mud, the grandeur of the remote country houses suggesting lifestyles so different from the city lives Jess and I know, and the slippery sometimes treacherous icy farm tracks which men in heavy Land Rovers ploughed through with little regard to our presence. The memory of the man's slightly peeved manner lingers in my memory of the walk too – a manner which seemed to say, "This is a Monday, a morning for business, a morning for locals, not city types lurching ill-equipped along farm tracks and across stiles and fields for recreation." And it's true that because of the underfoot conditions of the ground, we didn't just walk, we stumbled and fell, and we squawked and swore so that consequently there wasn't so much a conversation during the early part of the walk as a battery of noisy protest.

And there were things incredibly special about the walk, the other-worldly grandeur of the Balcombe viaduct soared above us, an endless repetitive row of brick arches, an awe-inspiring reminder of a solid material world, a monument to the innovations and toil of the Industrial Revolution. Now, I reflect, the world feels more flimsy, featherlike, a world built of pixels and not brick, and I think to myself that unlike the viaduct, these ephemeral building blocks of modern life break up easily, disintegrate before our eyes, leaving no solid trace of the lives we have led for future generations to gaze at or admire. It's a strange legacy for our age.

Figure 38: Balcombe Circular No 4

The mighty viaduct appears out of nowhere, like CGI in a film, it looks real and also unreal. We admire the brickwork and the symmetry of each supporting arc. I'm so busy looking at it and oohing and aahing that I fall in the mud.

"Don't look at me!" I shout at Chris, embarrassed to be seen to fail.

"You need boots!" she laughs.

I am ill-equipped. A croissant that is three days past its sell-by date and some very brown bananas are all I have brought, and my Nikes are ruined. My designer sunglasses keep sliding off my head when I stumble, and this is also causing Chris to pull silent for Chrissakes faces. How can I write a book about writing for recovery when I am so unsure of my steps, when I lack the basic tools for the job?

At the top of the hill, the promised marker is nowhere to be seen and I realise I have read the bloody instructions wrong. Two joggers in expensive looking kit stop and show us their GPS so we know exactly where we are and suggest we keep to the roads.

"Oh, I don't want to do that!" I say reluctantly.

"But you'll get wet," the jogger who looks like he might be training for a triathlon or the marines says to me patiently.

I look down at my sodden feet and muddy knees and then back at the jogger. "Bit late now?"

Chris and I amble down the hill where we hope to find the reservoir. It is unbelievably boggy, and I fall again but it is just so lovely out here and we are back on track, so I don't care. It suddenly seems inevitable to fall but also, to clamber back up, laugh and keep going.

Then there was the lake, about halfway round the walk, its flat blue surface a strange – almost artificial – phenomenon in the middle of the countryside green. The blue of the lake reaches down to touch the gravel path that frames its outer edge. The water is like glass, blue and grey, a place of peace and meditation. This is the axis of the walk, the place we aimed to get to, to walk around its clearly marked solid path. It is a realm of recreation. There are pleasure boats moored to its small boathouse, and local people walking their dogs around the outer perimeter of the lake. Whilst our presence would have been expected at the weekend there is a sense that in the week this place belongs to locals not to visitors. Being there on a Monday morning feels out of step, out of time with the rhythms of the place, with the pulse of the countryside.

I offer to take the map for a bit as Chris's hands are freezing. Even as it approaches midday, the frost is still evident and in the shade of the wooded perimeter, it must only be a few degrees. We circumnavigate Ardingly Reservoir whilst munching on fruit. The cold and the scenery are breathtaking and we hardly see a soul. I decide to take the detour on the map that offers excellent views of the water, and we start hiking up. We come to a little bridge, and I tell Chris that when I was a child, my dad used to read the Three Billy Goats Gruff every night at my brother's request.

"It's such a male book" she laments.

"I know and I never really enjoyed it. Maybe I should rewrite it for the book."

An idea for a woman goat who is sure of foot and a misogynistic troll blocking her way begins to grow in my mind and I think about the pleasure that rewriting myself as the evil queen in Snow White gave me in the last book. This is something I should definitely do, and I feel buzzed by the idea, our discussion and the walk.

Figure 39: Balcombe Circular No 5

The flat calm presence of the water and the evenness of the terrain underfoot after the boggy fields we have walked through is a welcome relief and allows us to refocus on our project and we make the effort to talk about new hopes for the future, about new beginnings, new starts.

All is as it should be, everybody is in their rightful place, even us as the epitome of town mice in the countryside, but then in the field near the viaduct we encounter a young couple. We exchange greetings, and I am struck by the odd combination of items they are carrying. The young woman holds on tightly to a furry rabbit, quite a large floppy one, and the young man is carrying a box of wine – an incongruous mix for a Monday morning. They seem to be on a mission. She is ill-shod for the soggy grass, wearing soft UGG boots that sink quickly into the ground, and his footwear also caves in quickly to the boggy grassland, but they don't turn back, they seem determined. I wonder what their story is. Somehow it seems sad, but I choose not to ask, not to inquire any further. Whatever it is, they seem even more out of place and incongruous than we do, and they unsettle me a little.

As we meet the reservoir path again, two women tell us we are almost back where we need to be and that there is a very good pub and tea rooms not far away. The cold is in my bones now and we haven't eaten anything apart from my mouldy banana. A cup of tea sounds the very thing. We talk about what next for the book as we climb some very steep steps back into Balcombe and I concede that the instructions were useful, even if I mucked it up, and that yes, I do need some sort of boot or waterproof shoe if we are going to write a book on walking.

From the distance of the following day, I reflect that if I am honest, what I remember about the walk was not the beautiful scenery but the sad sight of a dead deer that had clearly been hit by a car and ceremoniously moved by somebody behind a tree on the roadside. Efforts had been taken to make sure that no further damage was inflicted on its seemingly unmarked body, suggesting a sense of remorse or regret. This sight of death unsettled me, hovering in my imagination even now, the day after the walk, taunting my efforts to think of the new, the positive, which was the declared purpose of this walk. I make a conscious effort to shake off this melancholy air and conjure up other memories of the walk and I think that even though we declared this walk to be about new starts, new beginnings, it also turned out to be about how the new can feel strange, unfamiliar, and put you in the path of the unexpected, the unknown, and how strange and discombobulating that can feel. We are still finding our feet and are uncertain what we are striving for, personally and creatively, and it is these questions that come to mind because of the walk.

New walk, same journey?

When I read through my account of the walk, I feel annoyed with myself. This doesn't fit the plan for this chapter; this was meant to be a cheery and uplifting account of a new walk, a sign of my willingness to let go of the past, to look to the future and try out new activities, a move towards recovery. I am struck by the slight sense of foreboding running through it, and the focus on death. I realise that the reality is that my ambition for a creative recovery is still constrained by an ongoing sense of not knowing the answer to the questions, will I be okay, will I survive? I still feel stuck.

> *My interest in uncertainty is related to the present and the*
> *ability to assimilate surprise. We look for transparency and*
> *predictability in everything these days. There is a lack of trust*
> *about everything. We want to prove, to know, to be certain.*
> *There is an inflation of the value of certainty; we need the*
> *opposite. This is where artists can play a role.*
>
> (Cantor: 2008, p 21)

A book called *The Need for Uncertainty* (2008) about the conceptual artist Mircea Cantor, sent as an unexpected gift by my sister, lands on my doormat like a talisman, suggesting the way ahead. Its theme of valuing uncertainty makes me reflect that I am here walking and talking to Jess, not for a social outing or whimsical day out but because I believe that by spending time together, I will learn something about what it takes to accommodate my fears, to live with a sense of not knowing and give a name and shape to my creative recovery, and that in discussing our experiences, I/we will gain new knowledge, insights and perhaps a little courage too about what it takes to hover in this space of unpredictability. I flick through the rest of the book in a distracted fashion looking for more inspiration, my eye landing on this: "Artists are like sponges. Wherever you point it, it absorbs moisture. I am sensitive to the realities that can become the source of inspiration for a work" (ibid, p.22).

I picture a sponge filled with holes, which triggers the thought that perhaps if I allowed this sense of uncertainty to permeate my efforts, let it flow rather than try to plug the holes, it might make my creativity more porous and receptive rather than solid and repellent. I ask myself what would happen to my creativity if I simply allowed myself to embrace the fact that my recovery (health and creative) may only ever be partial and fragmented rather than whole and complete, to reflect the reality of the world I now inhabit? Could accepting the fact that I now make art from a different place, the place of uncertainty, allow me to embrace both my willingness to move forward without denying my fears and accept that this place is equally valid and needed. And later, when I make small paintings about the walk, images emerge of women crossing over bridges with billy goats gruff hidden beneath, women stumbling over rickety fences but nevertheless pressing on, determined to complete the walk despite their fears and doubts.

Figure 40: The Wolf and the Deer after Mircea Cantor No1

Figure 41: The Wolf and the Deer after Mircea Cantor No 2

Task

Think of a metaphor for your creativity (Chris has picked a sponge). Paint or write about your creativity using this metaphor and think about how this confirms or shifts your beliefs.

List of Figures

Bibliography

Cantor, M. (2008) 'If you hold your breath' in Cotter, S., *Mircea Cantor, The Need for Uncertainty.* Modern Art Oxford. pp.21-28

Whose voice is it anyway? Accepting our inner critic

Jess

In 2007 I ran a writing retreat with academics where we all talked about the voice in our head telling us we weren't good enough. It was a shock to hear that colleagues – some new like me, others mid-career researchers, and even internationally respected professors – all experienced bouts of extreme self-doubt and had an inner critic telling us we stank. As we swapped experiences and tools for dodging this censor, I found myself strangely comforted and also terrified that this voice might never go away. Back then, I was a brand-new lecturer with huge imposter syndrome, waiting for someone to tap me on the shoulder, smile politely and escort me from the campus. I had the same sensation two years later when my son was born and on leaving the hospital, stitched up and still high on drugs and euphoria, it seemed inconceivable that they were going to let me take him home. "You? Be a mother? To something as incredible as this? Don't be daft." the voice spat into my ear – the only part of me that didn't feel unreservedly battered at that point.

> *Your dastardly inner critic fires negative thoughts at you to persuade you that your core beliefs are facts. But thoughts are not facts, they are just ideas and like all ideas they need to be tested. So whenever I was attacked with one of my own unhelpful core beliefs or any of its derivative negative thoughts, I started weighing up the evidence for and against them. With time and effort, I started to realise that my inner critic was spouting nonsense.*
>
> (Ahmed: 2020)

I'm not sure I agree that the inner critic always spouts nonsense – sometimes for sure – but I have not yet found a way to make it magically disappear and I'm fairly sure I wouldn't want to. With hindsight, the voice personified the weight of responsibility I felt when charged with educating students and bringing up a child. I was never chucked off campus and I did take my son home – he's twelve now, still incredible – and I am strangely grateful to the critic for pressing into me how mighty those responsibilities were and are. Knowing when to listen to our inner critic and when to silence it is important, but those voices in our head shouldn't be ignored; instead, we should engage with them, speak to them, ask them what they want, tell them how they can help and when they can back away. A friend who has published extensively and says she has never suffered with writer's block is able to dismiss her inner critic by flaunting her successful career and the fact her writing pays the bills, but for those of us who feel more vulnerable about our creativity, or perhaps less professional or established as practitioners, ignoring or quietening the voice can be hard or worse, destructive to the work we want to produce and that nourishes us.

> At its most helpful, the 'Inner Critic' enables us to gain the 'objectivity' or critical distance from which we can see what is flawed or fine about our writing. This aspect of our inner world can help us see more clearly what works and what doesn't, what makes sense, and what doesn't. We might think of this as an 'Inner Muse'; as a benign inner source of support and inspiration.
>
> (Edwards: 2011, p.13)

Whilst running academic writing retreats, one woman said that the voice was always her ex-husband, another the voice of their mother and someone else the voice of a teacher from when they were small. For me, the voice was mine, but it was faceless and shapeless, just an omnipotent droning sound that, once it started, was almost impossible to switch off or turn down. Other people on the retreat agreed that the voice was their own, demanding that we listen and always present – sometimes out of sight but looming and judging or other times screaming out loud. Whilst on retreat, we drew pictures of how we imagined the critic to look and wrote it letters, asking it to be kinder, more supportive, quiet. Some of us thanked the voice for giving us that pressure and drive to get things done, for being a competitor we were compelled to face and beat, for always being there. This method, combined with time and experience, has helped me come to know my critic. I don't fear that voice the way I used to, and I have grown better at telling her – mine is a she if she has a gender at all – when I need her and when I don't. For me, it is always about 1 o'clock in the morning, when no matter what I say, how much I implore her, she won't shut up. If I trace back, the critic has always been there but when I joined the university, the pressure I put myself under (and that I really was under) was like giving her a megaphone, pom poms and unlimited caffeine. She was relentless no matter what I did.

A large part of this was that I thought I had to change my creative practice to fit in and feel validated in academia. Creative writing is in contrast to the objective, male, hierarchical style that academic writing still tends to privilege. I didn't want to collect data or develop expertise in some obscure area. I wanted to write and tell my students what that can be and is like. But when I suggested that I use my research time to complete a novel, I was told it wouldn't be relevant to my career. The irony that as a creative writing tutor I was told not to write creatively is still not lost on me. Speaking to colleagues, I began to realise that many felt the same way, unable to write vivid, personal, engaging work but instead compelled to produce pieces that journal editors deemed worthy and that were only read by a handful of people.

> *They (academics) started to question why university life had to be that way, why they had to be removed from their work, why only certain forms of discourse counted as knowledge, why they didn't feel more connected to those they studied, why their mind should be split from their body, why they had to keep their emotions in check, why they could not speak from the heart.*
>
> (Pelias: 2004, pp.10-11)

Separating head and heart in my writing was unnatural and stressful and it was only when I started work for my thesis that I realised there were alternatives and that I could combine critical and creative styles in my research – that is what this book hopes to do. Finding ways to restore our belief in what we do and why it matters is potentially a more effective way of arming ourselves as we come to face the inner critic. Don't deny them or imagine they might ever abandon us.

> *Writing is always rooted in something beyond language, it develops like a seed... it is intimidating.*
>
> (Barthes: 1968, p.20)

In my experience, being creative – in whatever style or medium – is an emotional, identity-related activity as well as a technical, craft-based one. Making is intricately linked to a sense of self (personal and professional) and is a way of expressing that self. Therefore, creativity cannot be taught in technical terms only. Any support and guidance for being creative must address personal experience and emotional processes that can leave us feeling exposed. "That is, any change strategy needs to be mindful of how fears can be managed and desires developed productively" (Lee & Boud: 2003, p.190).

I identify five specific obstacles that my inner critic puts up:

- Procrastination – *do anything but give time to your creative practice*
- Undermining my belief in my work and why it matters (to me or anyone) – *you are shit*
- Lack of motivation (creative block) – *why bother?*
- Telling me the work isn't good enough to share with anyone and prevents me getting feedback to help it progress – *they'll laugh at you and think you're a fraud*
- Inability to let go – *don't send it off! It's nowhere near ready!*

Does this ring true for you or would you change, delete, add anything? Try responding to your inner critic and tell it how it hinders you and what you know you need to do to work with rather than against it. Of course, for you, working with your inner critic might involve killing it, changing it, taming it and that's absolutely fine. Your experience with the critic is yours – own it! Art therapist (and dear friend) Tony Gammidge came up with this response:

Figure 42: The Inner critic – Tony Gammidge

And here's mine. Notice how I try and respond to the four obstacles my critic tends to focus on:

Dear Inner Critic,

How are you? You aren't as loud today as earlier in the week, is everything ok? I was angry that you told me this chapter wasn't ready, I am trying to deal with a million things at once and spending more time on this – when I have marking and meetings and being a mother to cope with – is not what I want to hear. You are right, it didn't need all those academic quotes chucked in. I need to stop worrying that my own story isn't enough and backing my ideas up with the words of others, it makes it really difficult to read and makes it seem like I'm hiding. I've gone back to it and edited most of them out. It's shorter, but more focused, and this feels right. I hope the readers connect with it.

I don't agree with you that showing my vulnerability makes me weak. I find it exhausting pretending to be expert, know-it-all, academic all the time. Who would even want to be or know that person? When people reveal to me their insecurities with their creativity, you never judge or damn them. Why are you forgiving and empathetic to them but so hard on me? I put the chapter to one side when you started getting louder, when I could feel your breath in my ear and the heat of your words on my skin. Thank you for not coming back at 1 a.m. There is never anything I can do at that time other than get emotional but we both know now: you can't break me. Better to come out between 9-5 p.m. when I might have time to listen and respond to what you say.

I've been working on it this morning and I am going to send it to Chris now. I know I have teaching to prepare and the online shopping to do but I wanted to give this the time it deserves so I got up before the kids and used the unusually silent space to get this done. Yes, yes, she will have comments and feedback and that's okay, because she never laughs or tells me it's rubbish as you seem to think she will. And even when she does suggest big changes and rewrites, I know it will be coming from a place of knowledge and respect so she will probably be right. And it will be a dialogue between us until we both feel it's right. It will be hard; it should be hard! It matters.

Are you resting at the moment? We've been here before – you pretend you'll go easy on me or take some time off but we both know it's an act and you know what: I'm glad. Don't go anywhere. I need you. Keep snapping at me, poking me, making me doubt. I will come back stronger. Those moments when I go quiet and your voice becomes the loudest in the room and I shrink until me and my words are almost nothing? Just so you know – when you've pushed me to a point when I promise to never pick up a pen or open my laptop or think or care or make? That's exactly when I'm going to come back and take you down.
Stay strong my friend,
Jess

Don't let your inner critic always win. Find a way to make the voice in your head work harder for you and maybe even support and motivate your creativity.

My inner critic now

She's still there. I've got older and more experienced but so has she. I imagine she feels quite neglected lately because often when we talk, I am telling her I don't have time to listen. I'm used to it but the pressure at work has intensified, the demands of students increased, and the volume of deadlines, emails and meetings never lets up. In my recent book (Moriarty, 2019) I talk about the significant rise in administration and pastoral duties that has disrupted the emphasis on teaching and research, changing the role of the academic from teacher and researcher to customer service provider. Cuts to funding across HE, but most specifically in the arts and humanities, have stunted research in these disciplines – and yet academics are still under immense pressure to produce research that is deemed to have impact by a government hell-bent on cuts rather than student and staff well-being and academic integrity. Academics have silently complied with pressure to do a lot, lot more for a lot, lot less, and the effects are palpable. A recent study by the Higher Education Policy Institute identified that the introduction of fees had turned universities into "anxiety machines" (Weale, 2019) where the numbers of students and staff being referred for counselling or to occupational health made it clear that there is a crisis in HE "where staff struggle with excessive workloads, precarious contracts and a culture of workplace surveillance" (ibid).

A report from the Education Support Partnership found that 40% of academics are thinking of leaving HE because they are stressed, anxious and disillusioned by the fear of rejection, heavy workloads and administrative pressures (Fazackerly, 2019). I have certainly experienced such thoughts, but I also know that being an academic is part of who I am and therefore, I have to find ways to negotiate with my inner critic and hold onto why teaching, writing and research matter. And they still do.

Although the inner critic remains, I rarely have time to give her the attention she craves. When I do, it's still at night when she reminds me what I have to complete the next day and the deadlines that I'm nudging back in order to make space for more admin and meetings. At 1 a.m. I am too tired to answer back and by then she is like a toddler, screaming and making irrational and unreasonable demands as loudly as possible. I let her scream. And then the next day she is exhausted and sullen, easy to fend off.

Do I still doubt myself? All the time! But I have people I can turn to who remind me I am okay, work to look back on that I am proud of, and a relationship with my inner critic that is more manageable now. I have accepted that she won't ever leave me and that doesn't scare me anymore. I sort of hope she does keep screaming, keeping me on my toes and hauling me back when I get complacent or take for granted the things I love about my job – working with students, research that I care about, writing that helps me come to know myself and my practice a little differently and a little better. Understanding my inner critic and checking in on her is part of that.

List of Figures

Bibliography

Ahmed, K. (2020). 'The inner critic: how to silence the negative thoughts that emerge in solitude' *The Guardian,* 8 April 2020. https://bit.ly/creativeP

Barthes, R. (1968) *Writing Degree Zero* (trans. Lavers, A. & Smith, C.) Hill & Wang

Edwards, D. G. (2011) 'Once more, but with feeling: Further thoughts on writing about art therapy', *ATOL: Art Therapy Online*, 2(1)

Fazackerly, A. (2019) 'It's cut-throat': half of UK academics stressed and 40% thinking of leaving | Lecturers | *The Guardian*

Lee, A. & Boud, D. (2003) 'Writing Groups, Change and Academic Identity: research development as local practice', *Studies in Higher Education*, 28, 2: 187-200

Moriarty, J. (2019) *Autoethnographies from the Neoliberal Academy: Rewilding, writing and resistance in Higher Education,* Routledge

Pelias, R. (2004). *A Methodology of the Heart,* AltaMira Press

Weale, S. (2019). 'Higher education staff suffer 'epidemic' of poor mental health'. *The Guardian*, 23 May 2019. https://bit.ly/creativeQ

Skipping past the inner critic: Image making and re-imagining

Chris

Jess sends me a retold story of the Greek goddess Hera; it is a dazzling piece of writing, re-imagining the tale from a personal perspective and, in so doing, challenging the phallocentrism and patriarchy which lies at the heart of much of these traditional tales. I love it and hope that it's included in this book. Jess's writing daunts me and my inner critic stirs in my gut and starts to slowly prowl around, looking for sport, looking for food and I oblige: "What are you doing trying to write, you're a dyslexic, it's ridiculous! You are an outsider, a pretender," it howls. I am familiar with the feeling, a plummeting of self-confidence, a loss of self-esteem when I shut down my willingness to try. The pit in my stomach is real, visceral, linking my thoughts to my body by a tightrope. How on earth am I going to write about my inner critic now, I wonder.

"I have no words," I whimper to Jess.

"You could paint your inner critic," Jess urges, not letting me off the hook.

That evening I sit down in front of the TV, unmotivated, and gather a few old newspapers from the last few days that haven't yet been used on the fire. I decide to start by making a quick collage of my inner critic, to try to get some image of it, so I can bring it into the open and at least acknowledge what it looks and feels like. I cut out images that I respond to in some way, and then set about sticking them onto a piece of paper. I am only half focusing on the task because I'm also watching the new series of *Killing Eve* which I find engrossing. I work quickly and by the end of the programme I've made a couple of collages and small sketches.

In the first collage, the beast in my stomach turns out to be a dinosaur or, more accurately, two dinosaurs fighting – or are they playing? It's difficult to be sure. Whichever it is, it feels like these long-vanished beasts are still here, seemingly revived and tussling in my gut, their slow lumbering movements causing my stomach to churn. A perplexing array of letters, numbers, and words, gathered from various newspaper crosswords and Sudoku puzzles, line up across the page alongside the extinct beasts. In everyday life I am careful to avoid these tests of mental agility because I consider myself too slow-witted to unscramble the clues that they provide, so I wonder why they are here in my collage now, taunting me. "What you write is nonsense, muddled at best," they chorus. Sometimes when writing I can feel like Mr Bean, the klutzy character in the 1990s TV series of the same name, played by Rowan Atkinson. I carefully read the material, gather my notes, think about what I want to say but when I look back at my efforts it makes no sense at all or bears little relation to what I intended to say and each attempt to claw it back seems to further mangle the meaning. Letters and words swirl. The final flourish is the dyslexic array of mis-spelt words, imprecise grammar and lost references. The collage seems to reflect this inability to grasp the words in the order or sequence that I need them, to tidy them up and make them presentable.

Figure 43: Surfacing the inner critic

Alongside this, a girl with enormous hands is stubbornly holding up a grey cloud hovering above her head with thin outstretched arms as if trying to prevent it from enveloping her in its misty shroud. Another girl is crawling on her hands and knees along the ground, trying to keep going, inching forward but without much conviction. "You'll never get there," she seems to say. It dismays me to see her there and I want to say to them "Let the rain fall, rest up. It will be fine."

In the ink drawing that came next, a girl is dressed in tatters, with arms hanging limply by her side, dangling inertly by visible threads from the same dark cloud. Wooden and deprived of life force she has become a puppet-like figure, waiting to dance to the tune of the litany of doubting and disparaging voices floating in the cloud above her. I find the symbolism almost laughable.

I chastise myself, "Surely you could come up with something more out of the ordinary than a cloud, or a puppet?" Critical, then, even of my inner critic! I notice that the ink drawing has some writing in the far top corner, handwritten notes I made whilst listening to the writer Naomi Klein talking on the news the evening before about the future post-Covid: "Where are we going?" she asks (Channel 4 News, 2020). What if I asked this question to my dangling girl, I think to myself? But then again, the question asks "we" not "you" so I wonder who this "we" might be? Perhaps it's all the girls in the images I have made? Perhaps it's the viewer? The answer is left hanging.

Figure 44: Dangling women

The image plays a vital role within psychoanalysis as both a mnemic carrier of lost meaning, as a translation into a rebus-like language system, in dreams, for instance, that can be otherwise deciphered, and as a screen, a displacement, a deception that, none the less, makes meaning possible despite censorship and repression.

(Pollock: 2007, p. 56)

Making images of my inner critic, making it visible, has opened up a space in which to interpret and debate this voice, not with a view to finding definitive answers or solutions but simply to explore the terrain it inhabits. What do I read into them? Certainly, the image I make can't be read simply as a straightforward representation of my conscious thought about my inner critic because as Griselda Pollock explains, "the book, art, the image does not just stage a story of subjectivity, it is itself a performative enactment with its own lapsus (a lapse) and, more importantly the imprint of the unconscious" (Pollock: 2007, p.58). By this, I understand that these images reveal both the thoughts and feelings about my inner critic that I am aware of but also pierce through to reveal aspects of my thinking and past experiences that have slipped my memory or understanding, that hidden reservoir of thoughts and feelings that nevertheless are guiding my actions. Of course, this representation of what is in the conscious/unconscious will be imperfect, fragmented, and partial because as psychology tells us, from the writings of Sigmund Freud onwards, getting to grips with all that lurks in the recesses of our minds is a challenge, unknowable even. This matters because I am aware that this marriage of thought that I am cognisant of, and the subterranean network of buried emotions and feelings, influence the way I respond to experiences of my inner critic in the present moment. Finding a visual language for this debilitating experience of my inner critic seems to be crucial because, without being able to see it, making the experience visible for myself, how can I hope to counter its voices or seek the support of others to do so?

In *New Maladies of the Soul* Julia Kristeva argues that "At this point in its journey, the new generation is coming up against what I have called the symbolic question" (Kristeva: 1995, p.210). For her, this is "a matter of clarifying the difference between men and women as concerns their respective relationships to power, language, and meaning". She continues, "this focus will combine the sexual with the symbolic in order to discover first the specificity of the feminine (le féminin) and then the specificity of each woman" (ibid, p.210). Kristeva argues that feminists "seek a language for their corporeal and intersubjective experiences, which have been silenced by the cultures of the past" (ibid, p.208) and urges the new generation of women, to use the arts to expand and challenge the existing symbolic order. She continues, "Along with psychoanalysis, the role of aesthetic practices needs to be augmented, not only to counterbalance the mass production and uniformity of the information age, but also to demystify the idea that the community of language is universal, an all-inclusive, equalising tool. Each artistic experience can also highlight the diversity of our identifications and the relativity of our symbolic and biological existence" (ibid, p.223). In other words, women are urged to use the arts, writing and artwork to create a symbolism that is faithful to, and comes from, their own experience, and because artwork is the result of personal artistic effort it will enable us to assert the diversity of our individual voices into the existing symbolic order, disturbing its architecture, creating new spaces that are reflective and therefore supportive of our experience.

However, finding a language of your own is challenging because we are immersed in a culture in which the signs and symbols that surround us already have their own connotations, and because any artwork reflects not just the time and place and circumstances in which it was made but also histories and associations of the signs and symbols it deploys (Pollock: 2007). In my collage, I have appropriated pre-existing signs and symbols (numbers, letters, ancient creatures, figurative language, gestures, etc) and varied their meaning so that they speak of my own experience as well as these prior associations, placing my inner critic in a dialogue with these pre-existing narratives and so complicating the representation of my experience.

Figure 44: Lines of flight

Flying is a woman's gesture – flying in language and making it fly. We have all learnt the art of flying and its numerous techniques: for centuries we've been able to possess anything only by flying; we've lived in flight, stealing away, finding, when desired, narrow passageways, hidden crossovers.

(Cixous: 1975, p.258)

After a short tea break and against the backdrop of the 10 o'clock news, with grim updates on the Covid crisis, I feel like something has shifted. My mood has lightened and the sensations in my gut are quieter, less intrusive. I begin to feel as if I want to move on and make a couple of sketches of my creative self now. A spirit of energy runs through me and encourages me to paint quickly. Once complete, I see looking at these new images that the debilitating blows delivered by the ancient beasts, the sea of meaningless letters and numbers and the grey clouds have gone, leaving only a girl in flight displaying a new sense of playfulness and freedom. I reflect that my earlier artistic endeavour to represent my inner critic in collage has helped alleviate those inner voices that left me frozen, unable to act and made room for something new, more optimistic, confident to emerge even if momentarily.

And if, as it does for me, the inner critic equates to a loss of self-confidence and self-esteem, we know from psychoanalytic writers that finding ways to represent these experiences of loss is crucial to allowing them to be first acknowledged, mourned, and ultimately overcome (Freud: 1917; Kristeva: 1989). In relation to these feelings of despair Kristeva argues that "Artistic creation integrates and expends them. Works of art thus lead us to establish relations with ourselves and others that are less destructive, more smoothing" (Kristeva: 1989, pp.187-188). Moreover,

> *On the contrary, the work of art that insures the rebirth of*
> *the author and its reader or viewer is one that succeeds in*
> *integrating the artificial language it puts forward (new style,*
> *new compositions, surprising imagination) and the unnamed*
> *agitations of an omnipotent self that ordinary social and*
> *linguistic usage always leaves somewhat orphaned or plunged*
> *into mourning. Hence, such a fiction, if it isn't an*
> *antidepressant, is at least a survival, a resurrection...*
>
> (Kristeva: 1989, p.51)

For me, making artwork that addresses the inner critic is a way of bringing aspects of those experiences that relate to feelings of loss and sadness to the fore and giving them presence and recognition in our culture.

As if in a dream my inner critic is now weightless, flying, floating, languid and free. In the first drawing she seems to be in the same slipstream as others heading her way and, in the second, she has wings, and her sense of direction is strong, purposeful, resolute. I stop there and enjoy her being there a while.

Talking to Jess and other women artists, I realise there seems to be a certain resilience, born out of experience, that quiets this inner critic. They recount similar tales of the experience of knockbacks and also a determination to get back on their feet and have another go, to not be deterred and to keep on working. Jess talks about this herself in her writing, acknowledging that experience has brought an ability to manage this critical voice. Hearing these stories of determination, peppered with ups and downs, and successes and failures, helps me understand that I am not alone with my inner critic, that there are voices other than my own, talking back to it, questioning it. I believe that these voices will improve our collective understanding of women artists' experience of the inner critic and the strategies they use to quell it.

Figure 46: Flying women

Task

Acknowledge your inner critic

- Accept your inner critic as a lifelong companion – how can you make this relationship work for you?
- Identify the specific obstacles your inner critic puts up and how they manifest.
- Draw or write a response to your inner critic that addresses these obstacles and how you intend to move past them.

Make a collage of your inner critic - Try not to listen to them telling you it's no good!

- Gather some old newspapers, magazines, scissors, glue and a large piece of paper or cardboard. Sit quietly and think about your inner critic for a few minutes. What does it look like, feel like?
- Cut out some images and words that you instinctively respond to. Do not overthink. Work quickly.
- When you have gathered a pile of images and words, make your collage. A collage is made in layers, with images and words overlapping and juxtaposed.
- Look at what you have made. It's an interpretation of your inner critic. What does it show you, tell you about your inner critic? What images, patterns, and ideas are evoked by your collage?
- Write about it. What have you learnt about your inner critic?

List of Figures

Bibliography

Cixous, H. (1975). 'The Laugh of the Medusa' in Robinson, H. (ed) *Feminism – Art Theory an Anthology (1968-2000).* Blackwell, p 635

Freud, Sigmund (1917) 'Mourning and melancholia'. In: Freud, Sigmund and Strachey, James: *On Metapsychology: The Theory of psychoanalysis: Beyond the pleasure principle, 'The Ego and the Id'* and other works, Richard, Angela (ed) (1991) Sigmund Freud 11. Penguin Books, pp.245-268

Kristeva, J. (1995) *New Maladies of the Soul,* Columbia University Press

Pollock, G. (2007) *Encounters in the Virtual Feminist Museum,* Routledge

Channel 4 News (2020) Channel 4, 3 March 2020

Chapter 5: Covid Diaries

Chris

Boris Johnson announces a complete lockdown at 8 p.m. on Monday 23rd March 2020. We are to stay at home except for essential trips to food shops and for a daily dose of exercise. All shops, except food shops, will shut. We should switch to online remote working/home working wherever possible. It's stark, unreal. Things that we have watched on television, which happen on the other side of the world, are happening here, and we aren't used to that. A slight sense of hysteria and stunned silence blankets the country. There are rapid and slightly bonkers exchanges of film and social media memes amongst my friends reflecting, I think, a response to the strangeness of the days we are living through. There are tales of people walking around their front room, running marathons on a balcony, in the garden, performing gigs in their front rooms. People are crazy and innovative. I am heartened by this, but this is not my response. I burrow down, take cover under the silence.

Some people respond creatively and with energy to the new dystopian scenario, but I need time to adjust to this new way of being and to reflect on what this means for our book. I have already experienced one setback and I am aware that we are only in the foothills of this pandemic, I will have to adapt, make more changes. And most significantly for Jess and me, meeting with people outside your own household is prohibited. We must find a new way to talk about our project. Will this situation give our project new significance or make it redundant? I am open to both possibilities because this crisis reminds us to focus on what matters, what makes a difference, what helps. Almost immediately we cancel our plans for more walks. But then what? How to fill the void, the space left by these cancellations, these postponements? What do we do when the tectonic plates shift?

Reverie and daydreaming as a form of personal reflection that supports creative practice

> *...time spent collecting one's thoughts, time to work*
> *undisturbed. This is space for contemplation and reverie. It*
> *enhances our capacity to create.*
>
> (bell hooks: 1995)

Figure 47: Floating

It's early in the year but the day is hot, the sky blue, and the sea calm. A perfect storm. I'm already warm from cycling the five miles from my home to Shoreham beach. No excuses, I tell myself. I would normally wait until June for my first swim, but this is week eight of lockdown and I want to feel the sea support me, embrace me, chill me, comfort me. I know that if I let myself off the hook and just sit on the beach, any initial feeling of relief will be swiftly followed by a sense of disappointment that will stay with me for the rest of the day. An opportunity lost. So, the sea beckons and a feeling of nervous excitement wells up as I don my sturdy swimsuit.

Figure 48: Looking back

I hobble across the strand towards the water's edge, my feet absorbing the first shock of the icy water. I freeze momentarily and make a strange involuntary noise but then slowly, very slowly, I inch in, giving my body and breath time to adjust. I look back briefly towards the beach and a woman smiles, and this small gesture of encouragement overcomes any lingering doubt. There are no sudden moves today, it is numbingly cold. Up to my waist now, the gentle waves making me unsteady on my feet and the moment arrives when I must launch myself and swim. This is it. I take a deep breath, and once in the water my breath quickens as I frantically swim against the cold and hear myself making shrieking noises, involuntary sounds of protest. I immerse my head, feel the relief of that icy grip stripping my head of thoughts, of feeling everything except the sensation of the sea on my skin.

Slowly my body warms, and my breath adjusts. As the cold abates, I swim steadily across the width of the beach. I feel exultant, alive, and energised. Another woman bobs up and down nearby.

"Isn't it fantastic?" she sings, and I beam back in acknowledgement.

This is joy. Certainly, it feels like an achievement to have made it past my own doubts, to be swimming.

I think of a four-part video installation (polyptych) I saw at St Paul's Cathedral in London by the American artist Bill Viola, called *Martyrs (Earth, Air, Fire, Water)* (2014). In the part of the polyptych that relates to the element of water a person dangles upside down by a rope with the water slowly rising around him, like the tide coming in. The fleeting memory of this image serves as a reminder of the overwhelming power and force of water, even on the calmest of days. Almost simultaneously another image drifts into my mind. A scene from a series called *Unorthodox* that I watched on Netflix, in which a Jewish woman immerses herself in the water before being married. "The immersion must be total, nothing to come between the contact between the skin and the water," instructs the mother (Unorthodox, 2020). The message of the ritual seems to be one of cleansing and rebirth, and I reflect that I feel that spiritual quality each time I immerse myself in the sea – that sense of washing away the day, casting off cares to be carried away like flotsam across the vastness of the ocean.

After a while, I start to float on my back, resting on top of the waves, gazing at the wisps of clouds as they pass over the otherwise clear blue sky. My mind is emptied of thought except for the sensations and pulses of the water that support my body and cool my mind. It's bliss, a delight, to abandon myself to the elements, to let go. I fleetingly think of the image of Sir John Everett Millais' grief-stricken *Ophelia* (1852). Driven to despair after her lover, Hamlet, kills her father, she falls from a bough over a river whilst collecting flowers for a garland and drowns. In the painting she is floating on her back down the stream, seemingly unaware of the danger posed by her heavy clothes "...Till that her garments, heavy with their drink. Pull'd the poor wretch from her melodious lay. To muddy death" (*Hamlet*, Act IV, Scene vii). But just in that moment she is pictured, she is content, singing gently to herself, oblivious to danger.

It dawns on me that I am numb now, even warm, a sign that I need to get out of the water before I lose all feeling and get hypothermia. I swim reluctantly back to the shore, readying myself to ti toe across the punishing pebbles to the spot I have marked with a towel. As quickly as I can, I get dressed, comforted by my woolly jumper and old jacket. I lie back now on the warm pebbles and as I daydream the cool of my body meets the warm embrace of the thin sun.

After a while, my thoughts drift towards memories of being on holiday with my family, half-remembered glimpses of sunny days lingering in my mind and then moving on like the passing clouds. With these, comes a feeling of hope for a future holiday to replace the one that has been cancelled due to the virus, a holiday that will happen at some unnamed time to some unnamed destination. I picture a joyful gathering of kin. But my mind does not fixate; I am calm, accepting.

That evening at home I make two quick sketches of my trip to the beach. The first is of the moment I turned to look back at the beach and was cheered on by the unknown smiling woman, reaching back for somebody to witness my swim, affirmation that what I was doing was not nuts. The second is my memory of the moment when I have overcome my own doubts and bodily resistance to the cold and just float on top of the gently rippling waves. A sense of achievement. Letting go.

Reverie and the creative process

> *Women's need for uninterrupted space, undisturbed space, is often more threatening to those who watch us enter it than is the space, which is a space of pure production, for the writer when she is putting words on the paper, or the painter, that moment when she takes material in her hand.*
>
> (bell hooks: 1995)

And yet taking this time, these moments to allow the mind to relax and wonder is still something that I often feel I should not do, inwardly chastising myself for being unproductive and time wasting, not writing, not making.

And of course, as bell hooks reminds us, finding this time is complex, given that many women feel "utterly overextended" already by the effort of making money, looking after family. So, finding the time to focus on the writing and the making, let alone moments alone, moments of reverie and contemplation is a challenge, laughable even (bell hooks: 1995).

When I am feeling kinder towards myself, I know that although unfocused, this day spent getting to know my own inner landscape is not wasted but rather an essential interlude and part of my creative process, providing space for me to get reacquainted with myself, to check my bearings and allow hidden thoughts and feelings to surface. It is after these moments of contemplation and reverie that I often find a renewed focus and impetus for work. The day after the swim, there is a sense that my inner landscape has sorted itself out behind the scenes so to speak, rearranged the props for the next scene after the interval, and I work steadily on a set of paintings I have neglected for too long. Later, a couple of these paintings are accepted for the Discerning Eye 2020 exhibition and an artist friend seeing them comments that the paintings seem calmer and more serious than anything else I had produced recently. I believe that the mood and intent that I brought to the studio that day after the swim helped me in my creative work.

Figure 49: After JMC, No 1

This kind of personal and singular intimacy interests me and the kinds of activities that capture the journey inwards and outwards from oneself – autobiography would seem to be too linear a term, as if it were predicated on a type of chronology; I'm thinking here of the wanderings of reverie where the present and past co-exist, where reflection offers up poignancy and understanding that might otherwise be buried.

(Talbot: 2017, p.196)

These moments of reverie, as a form of personal reflection, are an example of what the artist Emma Talbot refers to as "an inward intimacy with oneself" (2017, p.196). This offers the opportunity to get to know the "irrational mechanics of our inner lives: those questions that hang in the air unanswerable – the unconscious triggers that ignite unexpected responses, my hopes, dreams, fears and love" (ibid, p.205).

I believe that such incidents of reverie serve to complicate and enrich the narrative relating to my autobiographical experience, mapping onto the chronological events and facts that shape my life my dreams and memories.

According to Ana Luísa Pinho et al, there is empirical evidence gathered from MRI scanning experiments with pianists that two systems govern our creative responses to problem-solving: the "extrospective and introspective neural circuits" (2016, p.3052). These circuits work in complex and interrelated ways so that creative thinking can be discussed in terms of the interaction between these two forms of cognition. Reading this material, I find it complex territory but am nevertheless intrigued by these scientific efforts to understand how creativity works in the brain. I take from these studies the broad idea that the 'extrospective circuit' is associated with a use of explicit organisation of our behaviour and is related to goal-setting, planning, selecting between options, etc. – behaviours that are in turn governed by our subjective conscious thought, intention, and sense of agency (ibid, 2016), in other words that part of our cognition that we deploy in a knowing way in creative problem-solving. The 'introspective circuit' is related to our memories and emotions and is concerned with the elaboration of affective meaning, and our ability to appropriately and spontaneously retrieve and access information in our unconscious and use it in our creative processes (ibid, 2016) and it is this part of our cognition that is relied upon more extensively in skilled creative problem-solving, allowing us to access our expertise in a spontaneous and instinctive manner. Furthermore, it is this introspective network that has the capacity to override habitual or uncreative ways of working and supports spontaneous and associative thinking (ibid, 2016). Beaty (2016) builds on this, asserting that reflective strategies such as daydreaming, mind wandering and future thinking may be effective in strengthening our creative capacity. In other words, time spent letting the mind unravel, unwind, and roam creates the potential for our creativity to override our habitual responses to the goals and tasks that we set ourselves.

> *Work for women artists is never just the moment when we*
> *write, or do other art, like painting, photography, paste up,*
> *mixed media. In the fullest sense it is also the time spent in*
> *contemplation and preparation. This solitary space is a place*
> *where dreams and visions enter and sometimes a space*
> *where nothing happened. Yet it is as necessary to active work*
> *as water is to growing things.*

(bell hooks: 1995)

If these moments of reverie and contemplation are essential to the creative process, we must take care not to iron them out in favour of more tangible goals. From my own experience, I would argue that time spent letting the mind unravel, unwind and roam is essential to the creative process, allowing me to make work that comes as least in part from that hidden terrain and to let go of the need to produce an output that is related to more tangible goals.

This time is not lost, but well spent and is embedded in the final works I make in the same way as the time I spend in front of the canvas or on the computer. As hooks writes,

> *Women artists cannot wait for ideal circumstances to be in*
> *place before they find the time to do the work we are called to*
> *do; we have to create oppositionally, work against the grain.*
> *Each of us must invent alternative strategies that enable us to*
> *move against and beyond the barriers that stand in our way."*

(bell hooks: 1995)

There was a time when a busy working and family life meant that finding time to make artwork was challenging and I feared claiming too much space and time for my creativity would signal that I didn't care enough about these other aspects of my life. With hindsight, even though I always felt like I didn't have enough time, this was a very productive period in my creative life, my artwork constantly referencing the maelstrom of my busy working and family life, with portraits of the children, the dog, the houses we lived in, generated at the same time as experimental works that were part of the art courses I had signed up to. Things have changed for me now my children have grown. I have more space for making, no excuses, so in theory I should be steaming ahead. Yet in truth, now that my life is quieter, making time to be creative requires more of a conscious effort on my part. The barrier is no longer time, but the diversionary activities that take me away from the studio and my creative work. Creativity is hard work, as well as rewarding, and time for self-reflection is more important than ever because it is these moments that help bring me back to my creativity, armed with new plans, new possibilities, new ways of seeing that excite and refocus my efforts.

Task

Value time for reverie

There are days when I am unable to make art or write because I feel mentally or physically tired or simply because, as Virginia Woolf describes, "a cloud swims in my head preventing me thinking things through or doing anything in any useful way" (Woolf: 1953, p153). On those occasions I have found that is important to allow myself to go off and do something different, a walk alone, an indulgent afternoon kip on the sofa, a moment staring out of the windows, a swim in the sea to allow my creativity to retreat and hibernate for a short while, to rest and to make space for my mind to wander away from its focus on purposeful activity and daydream and unravel. If I allow myself this time, these moments of brief or prolonged reverie, I find my creativity often returns with new impetus and gusto, sometimes making me bolder, braver and more certain of what I am trying to achieve.

Take time to consider the following questions:

- How do you relax and unwind? What activities do you find restorative and restful? This could be walking, watching a film, just sitting watching the clouds float by, fishing, swimming, dancing – any that gives you an opportunity for solitary contemplation and reflection.
- Make time to do this activity or try a new one.
- After this restful interlude, set yourself some new goals for your creativity. Do you notice any difference in your decision-making in relation to your creativity if you allow yourself this time to relax and unwind?

List of Figures

Bibliography

Beaty, A. U. et al (2016). 'Personality and Complex Brain Networks: The Role of Openness to Experience in Default Network Efficiency', *Human Brain Mapping,* 37, 2, pp.773- 90

hooks, b. (1995). 'Art on my Mind: Visual Politics' in Robinson, H. (ed) (2001) *Feminism – Art Theory an Anthology (1968-2000).* Blackwell. pp.125-132

Bill Viola: Martyrs (Earth, Air, Fire, Water) (2014), St Paul's Cathedral (permanent installation). https://bit.ly/creativeS

Talbot, E., (2017) 'Overstepping the boundaries: notes on intimacy'. *Journal of Visual Art Practice,* Vol 16, No 3, 195- 212 pp.195-212

Pinho, A.L., Ullen, F., Castelo-Branco, M., Fransson, P. & De Manzano, O (2016). 'Addressing a Paradox: Dual Strategies for Creative Performance in Introspective and Extrospective Networks', *Cerebral Cortex,* 26, 7, pp 3052-3063

Woolf, V. (2012). *A Writers Dairy: Being Extracts from the Diary of Virginia Woolf.* Persephone Books

Unorthodox (2020). Directed by Maria Schrader, produced and created by Alexa Karalinski and Anna Winger, Studio Afterlife

Reclaiming Stories

Jess

I have slowed down. Even the way I wake is unrushed. No scrambling through the midweek routine of emails, putting the washing on, emptying the dishwasher, bringing in bins, checking the news, Twitter, Facebook, stretches and sit-ups, looking coiffed for work, all whilst barking commands about breakfast, spellings and clean football kits at the kids before we've even left the house.

Leaving the house? We haven't left the house together in a car since this started. We haven't gone faster than 5 mph in four weeks. When we do leave, it is to walk the neighbour's dog on the downs where we can keep our distance from other families and elderly couples, to take the air and feel grateful for where we live. As we navigate rabbit holes and badger setts, we talk about the things we miss and what we hope will stay the same. My children's chatter mingles with the bleating of newborn lambs and skylarks and, more and more, the list of what they long for becomes less and less. I have already started to feel guilty about the mother I will become again when this is over: the manic plate spinner keeping everything up, my dial less attuned to who they are and what they need. Or perhaps this is too hard? They are so much a part of me that when I hear of parents in lockdown without their children, it makes me feel afraid.

They are bonded to each other, building dens and playing games, asking me to help them bake and make, resisting when I ask them to stop filming Tic Toc videos and join me in a dance class or PE session. Joe Wicks is our new friend. We talk to the screen every day as if on Zoom or MS Teams or some other platform where we meet our flattened friends. My daughter built a den on day one and continues to do football drills with her mates via HouseParty and WhatsApp. She sleeps until ten or eleven and I am reminded of the baby she was: peaceful all day and awake all night, feeding economically when she needed to and always with a slightly wild eye. My son would feed and feed and feed and needed holding and loving all the time. When he came home from school – perhaps his last ever day at the junior school he loved – he lay on the sofa, buried in my arms and asking for cake whilst his sister set him up on Google Hangout so he could talk to his class. He was knocked sideways, twitching and anxious, asking questions and doubting the answers that we couldn't swear to. Their older brother is in lockdown with his mother in Kent.

I tell him to wait a few more weeks before driving to see us and he resents me for it, almost as much as I resent myself. Fifteen years of consistency and commitment and when he needs us, I turn him away. I promise to make it up to him with holidays and a spa weekend, knowing that when this is over and we think about this time, this pushback is what he will remember.

I don't write. I read the work of anxious students and give gentle feedback rather than critique. I give out my phone number and hear myself pour sympathy down the phone like sugar, trying to sweeten what tastes sour – is £9k a year fair or right for an online seminar taught by a tutor who keeps saying, "Is this on? Can you hear me?" I hope the government will end fees and scrap student debt. Clapping for the beleaguered NHS seems a distraction, helping us to forget that our government made bad choices and wrong decisions that cost people their lives. Now they praise the institution they have been systematically dismantling for years and give tax breaks to Richard Branson who refuses to pay his Virgin staff and will probably end up buying our broken health service. Bile rises in my throat when I check the news, mingled with a shared grief for the women and men who have given their lives so the rest of us might be safe and for those who continue to die because our Prime Minister laughed and told people he was still shaking hands when he should have been telling us to stay at home and worry.

I am grateful for my husband. Grateful that he is as fastidious as I am, that he buys a new vacuum cleaner when lockdown starts and I tell him ours is broken. In our privileged life before, we had a cleaner who is currently unable to work and doesn't meet the criteria to claim furlough. In our privileged life now, we have a device he wields like a sword: defeating cobwebs and dust like the hunter gatherer I know him to be. He discovers he is a natural home schooler – inventing ways to get the children to study and motivating them with new methods of learning. His commute to Gatwick and back is not missed by any of us and he paints the decking, mends gaps in the plastering and feeds us with dishes he learns from Jamie Oliver. I realise he has become a nurturer, evolved as a man who cares rather than runs away. He is amazing and I tell him this while I search for online delivery slots and plot ways to treat my family in the new normal: deliveries of vegan sweets, fresh bread, goalposts, a table tennis set, and real ale arrive like magic – gifts to ease the transition into our new way of being.

We walk across bridle paths to my parents' house and talk from the end of their driveway about what we've done and what they can do to make the time go faster. My dad has started baking and watching online theatre and concerts. Tonight, The Boss (Bruce Springsteen) takes to the stage on YouTube and the National Theatre puts on shows worth dressing up for and we all gather round the TV in our finest gear to see an Italian farce. No last train back to Brighton, no five-pound ice cream or eight-pound glass of wine. No one even notices that I have my slippers on under my posh dress. It is privileged, middle-class bliss. My mum escapes to the stable twice a day to hay and horses. Her immune system is very low after years of urticaria and we worry about the virus hitting her hard. I fight the urge to parent her and request she stay home, knowing she fears her mental health collapsing even more than falling ill.

Most of the time, in our suburban bubble, as multi-coloured and uplifting as the one in Oz, I feel lucky, content. My family are safe and well and we have food and a happy home to hunker down in. I am not trapped with my domestic abuser, or unable to stock the cupboards because we've lost our jobs; we are not sick.

And then I see news of a 13-year-old dying alone in hospital, the names of the nurses, doctors and patients who are no longer with us, and the headlines proclaiming that our government is winning the battle against the virus from the east and I don't have the words to reach far enough into this time or the capacity to think forward to another time when things will have changed.

I decide that what I must do is write something else, another story of another time and place. Rewrite and remake myself.

Myth and Remaking

In previous work, I wrote about the shift in HE to a neoliberal agenda and how problematic (for some) the driving force of valuing students as customers, and staff as service providers, had been (Moriarty: 2019). I feel a responsibility to create storied, queer and wild spaces in academia that value and encourage other ways of being that challenge and resist dominant academic discourse. I can live within the bureaucratic and hierarchical constraints because the process of storytelling enables me to imagine and then make real a more creative and human HE where the nomadic academic is welcome to pass through and their knowledge valued. Autoethnographers strive to be "inclusive without delimiting" (Gingrich-Philbrook: 2003). and try to "remap the terrain" of autoethnography and queer theory without "removing the fences that make good neighbours" (Alexander: 2003, p.352). I identify autoethnography as a methodology that gives permission for a way of being in HE that values personal and evocative storytelling as Adams and Holman-Jones describe:

...work that simultaneously imagines fluid, temporary, and radically connected identities and that creates and occupies recognisable identities. Such work views identities as relational achievements: manifestations of selves that shift and change, that must be negotiated and cared for and for which we are held personally, institutionally and ethically responsible... Such work disrupts taken-for-granted, normalising stories and posits more open, more free, and more just ways of being in the world.

(Adams & Holman-Jones: 2011).

In *Wilding*, (2018), Isabella Tree acknowledges the detrimental effects of intensive farming on the Knepp Estate and critiques the pressure on farmers to over-produce so that the public can over-consume. She describes the impact of farming on the ecosystem at Knepp, but more broadly on our planet. Tree provides an insight into her own part in this massacre of hedgerows and biodiversity, and how the dominant narratives of produce and grow at all costs blinded her and her husband to what was happening at Knepp and what was being lost, in some cases forever. She describes what happened as a sort of sickness infecting the landscape and her conscience. Her beautiful book reminded me of Frank's guidance for people wounded in body and voice, "They need to become storytellers in order to recover that voice" (Frank: 1997, p.xii). In the way that storytelling helped me to reinvent my place in education, so too it helps me find a way through the Covid-19 crisis now.

I have re-storied myself as Hera who adopts the Hydra – the hideous multi-headed beast in Greek mythology (see below). This method takes me away from my normal writing practice, but I realise that the monster represents several themes for me – my creativity and also the time we find ourselves in – and I realise that I need to live with the monster rather than deny its existence or pretend I can kill it.

Hunt argues that by fictionalising our own autobiography, the writer is able "to move beyond entrapment in a single image of herself and to expand the possibilities for self" (Hunt: 2000, p.75). Walking and talking with Chris has made me see why rewriting Hera's story matters and how this process of adapting myth and restorying the self might be useful for others experiencing tremors in how they live, how they work, and how they make. This process of telling and sharing of stories might help others to feel better connected to each other, to colleagues and also to themselves. For me, this way of working offers a more intuitive and empowered process that is feminist and a part of the collective resistance to dominant male, hierarchical values that continue to prevail. This method can and will help to engage us in a dialogue beyond the self and with others in an embedded and holistic way, learning from and perhaps even benefitting one another.

***

Hercules did not kill my Hydra.

When Typhon first brought Hydra to Olympus, I thought her abhorrent. She was only small but two of her heads were already fully formed, grooming or harassing one another as she tumbled round court, forcing even Gods to move. It annoyed me how Zeus pitted all of his children against one another and worse, how they all succumbed. I couldn't remember the last time Typhon had come all this way to see me. I had tried to make friends with Echidna but she refused to leave the cave and the sunlight made Typhon's scales dry out which sent him into rages that could last for days, so now I hardly saw him at all. Sometimes I went years without seeing any of my children. When the opportunity to see them did arise, even in court and attempting to win favour with their father, I felt compelled to stay. Unsure of what role to play and hiding at Zeus's side, watching them please him, the way we all pleased him, never pleasing ourselves and rarely basking in the glow of his favour.

"Why have you brought it here?" Zeus asked, kicking the creature away as she tried to curl around his ankles.

"My lord, this child will be a fearsome adversary when she is grown, and she is one of a kind, unique."

Hydra rubbed against her father for comfort, but he recoiled.

Picking the babe up, Typhon held her to Zeus, "Watch my lord."

Typhon swiftly bit one of the creature's heads clean off its body, as if it were no more than an eel, and threw it back to the floor.

"Stop!" I cried, as the remaining head whimpered, sniffing, and licking the gaping wound.

The bloody stump pulsated. Slowly, two more heads emerged where the first one had been, both cawing and spluttering as they became whole. Even Hermes, who had seen so much of the world, stopped still, the court all turning to see this mighty and novel gift. The three heads wound about each other, sounding themselves out. The body moved with certainty, but the heads all displayed different characteristics, like triplets. One was shyer than its siblings, tentatively sniffing the air and holding back when the others feasted or fought, trying to stay out of the fuss. One was the loudest and the busiest, darting forward and checking all around for adversaries and often spying food or entertainment first.

126

But the middle head, the largest and the remaining original, was already the leader, commanding which direction they all followed and gazing at its audience as if judging them all. And this one's bright eyes kept coming back to me, locking me in her sights without any obvious fear. At first it was unnerving, but I found myself compelled by her, mesmerised by such a haughty stance and obvious power. Ugly as the thing was, she reminded me a little of how I used to be before Zeus bested me. Before I began to hate as deeply as I now did.

"Does its mother know you've brought it here?" Typhon looked at Zeus as if the sound of my voice had no effect.

Affronted, I moved towards the Hydra, "Stay where you are Hera."

Zeus put his hand on my arm, his fingers circling my wrist as a warning,

"Get off me," I hissed.

Zeus's grip tightened until I thought the bones would snap. I stifled a yelp and the Hydra halted at once, each head turning in unison and edging towards me as if concerned with what ailed me.

"Back beast!" Zeus growled and raised one of his huge fists as I had witnessed too many times before.

Hydra cowered but held her position, the middle head remaining fixated on me. I was anxious that this would only make Zeus angrier; he always detested any undue attention that was not focused solely on my looks. I went to usher the monster away, but he still had me in his other hand, the pressure almost unbearable but not unfamiliar either. Suddenly, Athena clapped her hands, delighted as she often was found to be.

"Father, let me have the beast!" she cried. "I will set it to work in your honour."

Typhon's face fell, realising that the child he had prised from its mother would be nothing but a toy for Zeus's brat.

"This is no pet!" he shouted, "This monster is indestructible, it will be the most feared of all my offspring, maybe second only to me!"

Athena looked at Zeus, her eyes beseeching, and I knew she would have her way. She had always been his favourite and I nursed my wrist and waited for him to name Hydra as hers.

The eldest of the three heads had started looking for food to quiet the younger two, she snatched a chicken from a gold plate and gave it to the new born pair to fight over, saving none for herself. While Athena made her case to Zeus, I knelt down and reached out a hand to the savage. The leader fixed me with a stare and moved in my direction so fast that, for a moment, I thought she may try and eat my fingers but instead she pressed her snout against my palm and wound her neck around my wrist which, whilst already healed, held the memory of pain my husband had inflicted. I waited while her breathing slowed and *matched mine and the other heads, shy at first, mimicked and soothed me. I fed them sweetbreads from my own plate and marvelled at how they worked together as one. I, who had been unimpressed by Zeus himself and needed tricking into his bed and onto his arm, enthralled by this serpent with legs. Hydra clambered onto my lap and settled, making a noise in its one chest like that of a common cat and despite myself, I stroked it and eased her into sleep.*

"Hera?" Zeus and the rest of the court were looking at me, Athena's cheeks flushed and Typhon even more dismayed. I was still furious with Zeus for silencing me in front of the court, but I knew anger was not the way to play this game.

"Yes, husband?" I ran my fingers down the neck of the elder Hydra and watched Zeus flinch.

"Would it please you to have the creature?"

Athena called out but her father shot her a look and she turned on her heels and promptly left. She knew that whilst her father's favourite, all he really cared for was himself and his own pleasure and it was I and I alone who gave him that. I was grateful when he lay with other women, even if he thought it would annoy me, it just meant I was less obliged to soothe his temper and remind him that he was the most powerful being in all the world. Keeping Hydra would cost me but I was used to that too.

Hydra grew. At first, I kept her in my room in case Athena was tempted to steal her away, but she was easily distracted and soon gave up on her fancy of having Hydra for herself. New heads birthed slowly over time, not out of anger and violence as Typhon had demonstrated but rather as it developed the need for one more. One took care of its domestic needs, one was wiser than the rest, one tried to please and dote on me, one, often dormant, had poisonous breath that it used at first to stun prey, rabbits and mice in the early days and then sheep and unsuspecting palace dogs when it became taller than a man. One night as we slept, I woke because Zeus was raging having stirred and found Hydra peering over at him.

"She meant no harm my lord. She merely wanted to see that you were sleeping soundly." I assured him, kissing his shoulders.

"She looked hungry!" Zeus snapped, rising from the covers. "The thing sleeps in here no more!" he warned, slamming my door.

Hydra slunk out from the corner, leapt up on our bed and curled herself tail to seven snouts. She seemed unaware of her bulk as over the years she evolved to be bigger than a dragon, bigger even than Scylla who continued to stalk the Strait of Messina, eating boatloads of sailors making their way from Sicily to Italy and still never sated or full. Servants fled as Hydra roamed Mount Olympus, casually feasting on cattle, sheep and humans if they bothered her. I found myself contented, watching her seven heads each embrace the novelty of their distinct personality and purpose, supporting one another and acting as one when they must. Occasionally there would be tension, one head wouldn't pull her weight, or another would want to travel where the others did not, but by and large they advised and encouraged each other, meaning that their initial tentativeness vanished, and they did as they all pleased. Sometimes she would go off and explore away from the mountain and I would fret that she might not return. Eventually she would come, nonchalant and pleased to see me. And I was happier when she wasn't lost to me. Spending my days finding ways to be noticed by Zeus, hurting him, battling with him, making up with him, took all my time but when Hydra came home, I would walk with her, watch her enjoy the pleasures Olympus had to offer. For whilst she was a fearsome predator, she was also kind, taking care of animals smaller and more vulnerable, ensuring the natural order of the mountains and plains below, revelling in the rivers and streams she played in and amusing herself with the company of her seven heads. Some nights, she would make a fire and curl around me while we looked into and beyond the sky and all the heads would listen to my stories of the stars and what had come to pass for them to shine there. When we returned the following day, I knew Zeus would rant and insist I remain at home and under his command for months, but it was worth it to feel free and as if something belonged to me.

Finally, Zeus insisted she be used to guard a door to the underworld near the Lake of Lerna in the Argolid. I did not beg for her to remain as I wanted, as she grew bored of the mountain and the tastes she could find there. She needed new challenges and adventures and I could not hinder her by making her stay. Instead, I travelled often to the doorway to see her and try its handle for myself. When I did, Hyrdra would implore me to come back, delighting me with some new trick or discovery that I would feel obliged to paint or write about in my journal, working on the shore of the great lake while she played and bathed within.

I was stupid not to think that Zeus would punish me for caring for her. Just as he had undermined me to my children, to see me ache when they rejected me, finally he found a way to strike, having lulled me into a false sense of safety at the lake. Sending Hercules to kill her as one of his labours was genius, I will allow him that, knowing that people would champion the false-god after I sent two snakes to kill him as a babe. The snakes were a stupid idea too. From a time when I thought Zeus capable of being hurt as I always was when he tested our offspring. I think of all the time I gave to wounding him, wanting him to feel as I did, vulnerable and alone even at Olympus where people always came to call. What a waste of my life! Combatting Zeus whose sense of entitlement and privilege meant the Fates always favoured him. I had known the snakes wouldn't kill Hercules, it was more of a threat to Zeus, but he had merely laughed when the infant killed them in his cot. I thought Hercules's survival was enough but clearly Zeus had waited, biding his time until an opportunity to hurt me through Hydra had arisen.

On the day Alcmene's bastard came to murder my Hydra, all I could do was cower in the shrub land, knowing that if I intervened, Zeus would not hold back. She tried again and again to outdo him but just like his father, Hercules was born with a sense that the world belonged to him. She couldn't understand his confidence in the face of her extraordinary form and it unnerved her. For the first time since I met her in court, I watched her falter and doubt herself. She was not used to such certainty and brutality and every time she changed tack, he seemed to mock her advance. Knowing she was doubting herself, I sent Cancer to torment Hercules but the crab's presence only distracted Hydra and whilst she swerved to avoid Cancer's claws, Hercules sliced off her first head, dipped his arrows in the venomous blood spurting from that neck, weakening her, and killed Cancer, urging his nephew to cauterise Hydra's wound before she could rebuild. And then my monster knew she was lost. And I could not bear to look into her eyes nor tear myself away.

Finally, when six of the heads lay still in the ashes of their battle, my Hydra gave one last surge, breathing her venom as she tried to force Hercules against the rocks on the edge of the swamp and end him as she was born to do. But the demi-god shifted, and without the ballast of her other heads, her weight and shape were new to her, she overshot, leaving her scaled neck exposed for him to bludgeon her lovely head. He hit her over and over while she screamed, blood from her veins soaking his tunic and lion fur until all was red. Even when the wailing stopped, he kept hitting her as if the momentum of his anger would not relent.

"My lord, she's dead," Iolaus crowed. "Come. Let's take her last foul head to Eurystheus and see the matter done."

"No," Hercules stopping at last, his arms hanging by his side as he surveyed the marshes and what he had done. "We bury it here. This is done."

It was all I could do not to rush out from the myrtle bush I was hiding in and shame him, for not just besting her but eradicating her, but I could not stand for tears and grief. He had taken a part of me I thought was indestructible, that would always be mine. I waited while he buried her leader head in wet dirt on the bank of the lake, no monument or ceremony, and left for the city and his banquet. People were already flocking to the centre wanting to hear of his bloodshed and power. As night fell, I used hands to dig her up, the mud and moss clinging to my dress as I worked, arms aching from the novelty of hard work, and still crying as I finally dragged her free of the bank and to where her body lay ruined in a clearing. The ardour it took to bring the parts of her back together tormented me. As a goddess, I was unused to toiling and sweating and once or twice thought to run away, back to Olympus and my life of plenty but also nothing, and I screamed at the sky when it was too much, and then came good again.

Her heads and lifeless neck were all together and, at first, I wanted to pray to the gods to make it right but then Zeus would have known what I was trying and sent me to the underworld with Hades or worse, taken me back with him. She was all there and I placed my hands on the eldest head and forced all my power into her. I called out in a voice I hardly knew to be mine and asked her to return. It was now dark and when my voice gave way and my legs began to fail, I curled against her neck and slept with my arms around her. Her blood drying, her body cold but, even then, animals of the lake and surrounding woods dared not approach us or feed on the pieces Hercules had left behind.

When the sun broke over the water, I was stirred by the sensation of a pulse through my body, the rhythm of a heart I knew as well as my own. My Hydra sat awake nestling my body with her fierce head, only one head had made it back and it pained her to see her sisters dismembered on the ground. I would not let her go as she tried to light each one before the scavengers took them as trophies or meat. She let me ride her as she adjusted to the weight of six stumps and the absence of her kin. Slowly we found our way through the swamp that morning, feasting on berries and water from the lake, finding places where we could hide and not be seen. I knew I would have to return to Zeus or he would send messengers to find me but I swore to Hydra that we would wait and bring him to his knees when I found a way.

She looked at me with her sad eyes. "What is it? Do you not want to kill the man who made you this way?"

Hydra looked again and I realised where her sorrow now came from, not for her sisters who had been slain, but for me.

Now my Hydra roams the marshes as she pleases, she swims in the deepest part of the lake and is content - mostly - only to be seen by me. Locals tell tales that she still lives and can be seen with a woman painting, dancing, telling stories to children about a fearsome beast who showed a goddess how she might be free. I have kept my promise to protect her from men and never use her for vengeance but more than that, I have kept a promise to myself. To look after my Hydra and the heads that have returned to us over time. To see my life with her as precious and important, feeding me and my need to be more than a woman warmed in Zeus's light. Hydra prevailed when all was hopeless. She is my solid faith in a world where gods always disappoint. Before I loved Hydra, I did not know the woman I was, but when my beautiful monster rose again, so once more did I.

Storying the Self

Storytelling can soften the edges of what we find hard or strange or new. In this way, in difficult times storytellers – in all their guises – can add oxygen and an aesthetic that is more optimistic and hopeful. The image of the phallocentric tower with the wild, climbing roses suits the storyteller in me: it disrupts the fairy-tale of Rapunzel (Grimm: 1812) and offers a way for the woman inside to climb down and escape. Working in this way we can reclaim myths – Hera's, Hydra's, Rapunzel's, mine – and offer other ways of being creative that are holistic and human. This process aligned with Hélène Cixous's *écriture feminine*, that involves dialogue and "free-writing, working around themes that emerge organically, intuitively and creatively, and tapping into a language of the body" (Cixous: 1976, p.141). This is with the aim of resisting traditional, male hierarchical discourse that continues to dominate life (Cole & Hassel, 2017). Working with Chris has made me feel supported and able to tell and reveal new stories that are transformative, ethical, safe – inspiring my creativity and helping me feel more connected to my practice and also helped me find a way of reigniting my momentum and pleasure with writing whilst in lockdown.

Task

Retell a story and make it your own.

- Choose a story you know – a myth, fairy-tale, urban legend, anything – and retell it using your chosen practice. Imagine yourself as one of the characters. How does this process help you to think about yourself and your creativity? What new observations do you make? If this way of working is new to you, what is useful about it? If you have tried this before then what can you do to make it more of a challenge this time round?
- Or write a story, make a short film, draw a picture, a photograph about a fictional character. What does this person look like, dress like, talk like, what do they want to say?
- What do you learn about your creative self because of these exercises?

Bibliography

Adams, T. E. & Holman Jones, S. (2011) 'Telling Stories: Reflexivity, Queer Theory, and Autoethnography', *Cultural Studies ~ Critical Methodologies*, 11(2), 108-116

Alexander, B.K. (2003) 'Querying queer theory again (or queer theory as drag performance)', *Journal of Homosexuality*, 45(2-4), 349-352

Bell, D. M. & Pahl, K. (2017) 'Co-production: towards a utopian approach', *International Journal of Social Research Methodology*, 21:1, 105-117

Chang, H., Ngunjiri, F.W. & Hernandez, K.C. (2013). *Collaborative Autoethnography*, Left Coast Press

Cixous, H. (1976). The Laugh of the Medusa (Cohen, K. & Cohen, P. trans.). *Signs*, 1(4), 875-893. The University of Chicago Press

Cole, K. & Hassel, H. (2017). *Surviving Sexism in Academia: Strategies for Feminist Leadership*, Routledge

Deleuze, G. & Guattari, F. (2014) *A Thousand Plateaus*. Bloomsbury.

Docherty, T (2012) 'Research by Numbers', *Index on Censorship*, 41, 674

Ellis, C. (1997) 'Evocative autoethnography: Writing emotionally about our lives' in Tierney, W. & Lincoln, Y. (Eds.), *Representation and the Text: Reframing the narrative voice* (pp.116-139). State University of New York Press

Facer, K. & Enright, B. (2016) *Creating Living Knowledge: The connected communities programme, community–university partnerships and the participatory turn in the production of knowledge.* Bristol: University of Bristol/AHRC Connected Communities Programme

Frank, A. (1997) *The Wounded Storyteller*, University Chicago Press

Gingrich-Philbrook, C. (2003) 'Queer theory and performance', *Journal of Homosexuality*, 45(2-4), 297-314

Grimm Brothers (1812) 'Rapunzel', https://bit.ly/creativeX

Hesse, H. (2017) *Narcissus and Goldmund*, Penguin Classics

Hunt, C. (2000) *Therapeutic Dimensions of Autobiography in Creative Writing*, Jessica Kingsley Publishers

Kelchtermans, G. (2005) 'Teachers' emotions in educational reforms: Self-understanding, vulnerable commitment and micropolitical literacy', *Teaching and Teacher Education*, 21, 995-1006

Marsh, S. (2015) 'Five top reasons people become teachers – and why they quit', *The Guardian*, 27 January 2015. https://bit.ly/creativeZ

McInally, F. (2019) *The Patient is Performing as Unexpected.* https://bit.ly/creativeAB

Moriarty, J. (2019). *Autoethnographies from the Neoliberal Academy: Rewilding, Writing and Resistance in Higher Education,* Routledge

Moriarty, J. (2014). *Analytical Autoethnodrama: Autobiographed and Researched Experiences with Academic Writing,* Sense Publishing

Moriarty, J. & Reading, C. (2019). 'Supporting our inner compass: An autoethnographic cartography' in Moriarty J. (ed.) *Autoethnographies from the Neoliberal Academy: Rewilding, Writing and Resistance in Higher Education,* Routledge.

Pelias, R. J. (1999) *Writing Performance: Poeticizing the Researcher's Body,* Southern Illinois University Press

Priyadharshini, E. & Robinson-Pant, A. (2003) 'The Attractions of Teaching: An investigation into why people change careers to teach', *Journal of Education for Teaching,* 29 (2): 95-112

Robbins, L. (1963) *The Robbins Report, Higher Education Report of the Committee appointed by the Prime Minister under the Chairmanship of Lord Robbins.* HMSO. https://bit.ly/creativeAC

Storytelling the Self: A symposium, 29th March 2017, Brighton University

Tree, I. (2018) *Wilding,* Picador

Troman, G. & Raggl, A. (2008) 'Primary teacher commitment and the attractions of teaching', *Pedagogy, Culture & Society,* 16(1): 85-99

Chapter 6: Passing Clouds – Keeping Creativity Moving

Final walk: Devil's Dyke to Ditchling Beacon and back

Chris

The day after this walk, Jess texts me the list of questions that we will discuss in the final section of this book, adding her reflection on the day: *that was bonkers but good like our friendship* and I laugh because that sentiment sums up the walk perfectly. We had chosen the route because we wanted to follow the suggestion of the women from the International Network of Women in Brighton and Hove who had named Devil's Dyke as their favourite place to visit outside of the city. "Go to the mountains to see the future," declares one woman enthusiastically referring to Devil's Dyke. I had been looking forward to this walk, imagining a brisk yet familiar wander across the top of the Downs, chatting to Jess about the book, art and life, and the night before it Jess had texted me the coordinates of a free car park, not far from the Dyke itself. All good.

I arrive at the spot, a little disorientated by the starting point which is not quite where I imagined it to be. I tell myself that it's all familiar landscape and besides Jess has the app with directions to Ditchling Beacon: all straightforward. The day is perfect for walking, no rain, no wind but cold enough to require gloves, hats and a winter coat, a proper December day. The first part of the route is exactly what I anticipated. We track the South Downs Way with views of the sea on one side and the flat plain of the Weald on the other. I breathe and we chat.

After a while, the route drops steeply down, joining scrubland that I recognise as part of the local rugby club on the edge of town. It is a place full of dog walkers in pairs with umpteen uncontrollable beasts, heaps of litter and the background noise of cars whizzing along the bypass. How did we end up here? Not exactly what I had anticipated.

"The app seems to have taken us on the most direct route for a car rather than a picturesque route for pedestrians," Jess muses.

Undeterred, we press on, confident that the walk will improve. We walk past a BP garage on the end of town and are forced to walk alongside a busy road and cross three roundabout junctions with fast and heavy traffic thundering past. This feels unsafe, dangerous even, but we press on, until we finally reach a track that points upwards towards the promise of green pastures.

Relieved, we stride swiftly on. There is speed, energy and intention in the way we are walking now, and we reach the halfway point of the Beacon. We mark our achievement with a brief pause, a swig of water, and munch on an apple before turning around to complete the loop back to Devil's Dyke. We don't linger, conscious of the immovable deadline of the school pick-up time. This part of the route feels much pleasanter, with fields of greenery stretching before us and we are enjoying ourselves now.

"This is more like it!" I say to Jess.

We are confident, relaxed, with nothing to deter us now. We see a sign to Devil's Dyke, but we decide to ignore it and go our own way, feeling that we sort of know the way. After all we can see Devil's Dyke in the distance, we can't go far wrong. For a while, this is fine. Our chosen detour takes us past a dew pond, with calm still waters nestled amongst gorse bushes, a welcome watering hole for the local wildlife one imagines, and along past the windmills, one of which has been converted into an impressive exclusive home with views across the landscape. The track drops steeply down towards a road that we need to cross to pick up the track back onto the Downs. Another road with speeding cars and not even a scrub verge that we can stumble along and it's a blind spot in the road. It's clearly dangerous but there is no other way unless we back track all the way to the windmills and pick up the recommended route and we know we are not doing that. Instead, we play a deadly game of chicken with cars hurtling past. Full of car fumes, we are relieved when we see the sign that takes us back onto a track up to the Downs.

I'd like to say that after this there is a gentle stride back, but the walk continues to throw up new challenges in the form of endless fields of cows. Normally I would do my best to avoid them but there is no other way today. I manage to get through the first couple of fields by asking Jess to walk on the side near the cows. This cowardice feels undignified but necessary. But then we come to a field that makes my stomach turn, it's steep uphill and the field is full of cows sitting and roaming right across the path and I am sure one of them is a bull. The entrance to the field is decorated with a warning label from the farmer about taking care when venturing through this field. I look for another way, but know there is none, I must go through them. I take a deep breath and walk swiftly, quietly trying not to look. And then out of the corner of my eye I spot an enormous goat with a huge set of horns, a proper Billy Goat Gruff, hanging out with the cows. He looks so incongruous there that it makes me laugh and fearful all at the same time. I see him as quicker, lighter more unpredictable than the cows. Even Jess who is impressively impervious to animal terror, seems a little apprehensive. But we race along to the top of the hill arriving out of breath, relieved, euphoric and slightly hysterical.

Figure 50. Loop

I'm getting tired now, and my shoulder is aching, a past injury exacerbated by carrying the backpack. We pass through more fields of cows, but it is as if my fear has run out and I stride on in the direction of the Dyke.

This walk has been odd, full of steep climbs and encounters with traffic and silent watchful beasts. As we approach the car, Jess points to an aeroplane doing somersaults in the sky above our heads. We watch it looping and diving and sweeping and whirling in the grey skies and there is something triumphant, magnificent about this display of mechanical daring. It seems like a fitting metaphor for our creativity. We watch as it falls into a death drop cutting off the engine and pitching towards the earth, I involuntarily hold my breath until it recovers and rises, and we both marvel and smile with a sense of relief. It is an exhilarating way to end the walk.

List of Figures

In Conversation – Why does this matter?

In this chapter we present an interview between the two of us – Jess and Chris – where we reflect on our experience of completing the book and using the methods, and consider our own creative recoveries. Jess's voice is italicised in order to distinguish it from Chris's.

Jess: Here we are after our final walk up to Devil's Dyke, and at the end of the book which started over a year ago now. What do you think has changed for you personally, creatively and professionally since we set out to complete the book?

Chris: I feel I have grown stronger, that there has been a strengthening of physical and mental health through the process of walking and talking and creating. I have moved from quite a low mood to something more robust. I do think that is a shift. Creatively there has been a shift because I took the decision to go back to the studio and that put me back in touch with my artistic community. I am creating on a more regular basis. Professionally, this has led to decisions to apply for exhibitions and competitions, and I have recently been included in the Discerning Eye Exhibition 2021 which was really encouraging. I might not have done that if I had not taken the decision to re-join the studio. So, I would say there has been a gradual shift in all those areas.

Having watched and worked with you during this time, I feel that your approach is much less tentative now. In the past, you've used the term hunkering down and I wondered if this felt more like a move to spring after a hibernation?

I feel more open to possibilities and open to trying things. Before there was a shedding and I didn't want to be carrying any excess foliage. Now I feel there is a willingness to try to have a go and to see where it leads with no particular agenda.

What have you taken from the process in terms of shifts and changes?

I think I have learnt that if you're going to be creative, you have to put it at the core, at the centre of your life and then things lead from that. I have developed a willingness to really listen to my inner instinct and to do what I need to do at a particular time, whether that's going for a walk or trying new media or exploring some other aspect of my life, I think that's important.

People coming to the book will hear that call within themselves, won't they?

It's very hard to live a creative life where you make that the centre of your life and make decisions that stem from putting that first because it can make you very vulnerable in terms of where an income comes from. The decision to put your creativity first is brave and, for some people, impossible because of commitments and pressures of family and professional life – like you Jess. But for me, the next step is ensuring that I put my creative life at the centre.

So I suppose for me, creatively what's changed is that when I started I had this idea that I might get a sabbatical to write the book, which I didn't, and then when Covid came, I thought that's fine because I'll have lots of time to write – as lots of people did when Covid started: I'll learn how to bake cakes, become a marathon runner, recreate the Sistine Chapel in my lounge – and actually Covid has decreased my time. Because I am physically more available, physically here for my children, my husband and, where are you going to say you are to your work colleagues? And to students? I am literally here (gestures to desk area) all the time, so creatively I think the book gave me a way of walking and writing and emphasised why these are linked for me, because walking is the only time I get for myself.

Do you want to say something about your dabbles with new media other than writing because, for me, that willingness to try new things such as painting, or a bit of sculpture has appeared over this period and marks a shift in your creativity?

The modelling thing I did because you made me. I didn't want to, which is funny because I'm always getting you to write rather than draw. The painting thing was an epiphany and I have painted since then. I'd always, always told myself I couldn't paint. I hadn't been allowed to paint for GCSE at school so therefore I could not paint. I found it liberating being in an art lesson and being told you need to think about colour, you need to do a palette like this, and then you need to look at that photo and you need to paint it and it was like yes, okay, I can do that because that is what I tell my students to do. And that made me think of the writer, Sonia Overall, and her practice during Covid. She does a lot of work on Twitter instructing people to take distance drifts and to do walks and to write about them. I find talking to her really inspiring for my own creativity and also professionally because I think she is somebody who has tried to do something on her own terms, she recognises the pressure to conform for work and the shift in higher education and education more broadly, but does try to carve out time and space to focus on the craft of writing and to link that to her academic work in a way that feels meaningful rather than a tick box exercise. I suppose that is something I have become much more interested in: how can I marry my creative and academic life? Can I bring them together more meaningfully?

139

And I would say that is an intention that has been there right from the beginning. Do you think because of this process you are any nearer to making time for your own creative practice in terms of your own writing outside academic outputs?

This book has been a labour of love. It's going to be an output, an academic output, but this is something I have really enjoyed doing; talking to other women and talking to you has definitely been nourishing. I really see a place for this work evolving and so I still think it's about marrying the two worlds together a bit more meaningfully and I feel that I am moving more towards that as a result of our work for this book.

What strategies do you have to make space in your working week for your creative work?

I still try to map out time and that is something I would definitely say to readers of the book, not to just say, "This week I am going to work on my creative self," but actually to say, "For two hours on Wednesday I will do this or on Monday I am going to spend 5 hours doing this and I'm going to invest in my creativity". I paid to do the art course, which I know was a luxury, but, because I had paid for it, I knew I was going to do it. And you can offset those things. Walking obviously is free and so even though the art class was a treat, I know I do other things to nurture my creativity that don't cost.

One of the things that is interesting about what you have said is that accepting a little bit of guidance, whether that is in the form of an art course or an app that gives you directions on a walk, can really support your creativity. It's not counterproductive that a framework, a structure, a commitment to start and finish something, is quite a good starting point.

Yes, and I think that is why we believe in the book as well isn't it? We want it to be a combination of gentle instruction and accessible tasks that we have engaged with ourselves to nurture and revive our creativity.

Have you had a creative recovery?

I think I had this idea that the book would be this kind of rebirthing and, realistically, it wasn't ever going to be that. The book should be transformational, but it would be wrong for us to promise that a creative recovery automatically means that you will publish your novel, or you will have an exhibition. And I think for me the recovery came with realisations about what I can do to support my creative life, how I can balance the professional and the personal and the creative and bring them all together.

On the 23rd December, it will be five years since I had a melanoma cut off my arm and then subsequently had various bits and pieces lopped off. My creativity is lighter now, I'm willing to take risks, I feel braver with my creativity. I feel braver applying for things, I feel like I have got a better sense of myself and that is going into my creative and professional lives.

Can you remember what your expectations were right at the start of this process?

I wanted to have more time to write, and I wanted it to feel different, and it does. We could not have predicted Covid getting in the way and that probably made me feel different again, but I feel that the model we have created with has been a massive part of me navigating this time. I could be feeling very different now – on the brink, anxious – but this process has brought me back from the brink and stopped me from feeling overwhelmed. It's guided, it's supported, it's in dialogue, so it provided a banister to the time during Covid. How about you?

I don't think for myself I had any expectations of this process. When we started off, I was pretty sure I would not go back to the studio. I didn't want to go backwards, and I think I saw returning to the studio as going backwards, but I no longer see it like that. Instead, I see it as a willingness to retrace my steps, as we did sometimes during our walks, and that has been helpful. Also, there is now some element of writing in my practice which I would never have imagined, and that has been fascinating.

I feel that you have changed so much in the last year. When you started this project, you were not a writer, you didn't want to write, were a nervous writer and now you send me writing four times a week – that has been a massive shift!

You have unleashed a beast!

I really have! But that is huge, your momentum with your creativity and your writing is huge. Also, I think you are such an advocate for our method because you really have done that thing of looking back to the people in your life who, historically, have helped you in terms of your creativity: your grandmother and your father and how they have inspired you creatively. And then the artists and the exhibitions and the creative communities that have motivated your work. And that remembering and reimagining through your writing has helped to restore you and now you trust in you and your process, and the writing and art has started flowing – your exhibition? This book? It is a time of spring for you.

Thank you for saying that, Jess. I think certainly there is more activity, what it leads to I don't really know but I think that will be interesting

And don't we both say that it's the activity that's important isn't it? One of my friends who is an artist said that it doesn't matter what people say, it doesn't matter what feedback she gets, she keeps going no matter what and now, when she feels creatively stifled, she goes out for a walk, or she'll go swimming in the sea, but she knows that this is the job, and she knows that she's got to just keep going. Even after her father died, there was the sense that, on the one hand she has to work, it pays the bills, but also that it was important to cast off doubts and keep making. Do you think your creative sense of self has shifted?

I am not sure how to think about writing now, I haven't yet fully absorbed it into my creative sense of self, perhaps that just takes time. I think my dyslexia is still problematic because I feel like I can only take the writing so far, and in the past, there is still a hesitancy, but I have learnt to enjoy it.

One of the things I thought works in terms of this partnership is that you have had time and the momentum to get writing done whereas I haven't had as much time but because you have been sending me work, I've been able to do the edits and proofreading which means that I am really having to focus on what you are saying and I do think that this has made this partnership stronger.

Yes, that way of working has been hugely important for me. I had to get over my slight embarrassment and I had to make a decision about that in a way because historically, with dyslexia, you hide it, or find strategies to get by, compensate, but I think this exchange of writing and redrafting has really helped us share perspectives and develop a creative connection, even in lockdown.

We did quite a lot of work on the inner critic, and I think that perhaps particularly in a year when people are feeling vulnerable anyway, whilst you don't just want people telling you that your work is brilliant and faultless, you do want supportive critique from someone you trust and where there is no power issue – you feel equal. Certainly, that's evident in the work that we do, we trust each other to provide feedback and that process is much more comfortable with someone you trust and respect instead of only having those dialogues with an inner critic.

What about your creative sense of self, how has that changed because of this project?

The art thing is interesting because I feel braver. 2020 has taught all of us not to take too much for granted and so telling myself that I can't do art, or I must not do art suddenly seems silly. Instead, the inner critic asks: why wouldn't you do art? And also it was an opportunity to spend time with my mum and it was creatively freeing. But in terms of my process, in terms of believing if I sit down and write I will get the raw material out and then I will share that and then I will do the drafting and redrafting and finish it, I am pretty happy with that process. I sort of believe in that process. And I have started walking with other people that I work with more and more as well now, out of need but also because of seeing that as a legitimate part of my creativity – walking, talking, the ideas start flowing, the breathing is different, the dialogue is different.

That's interesting. So are you saying that you have incorporated this process into other aspects of your professional life, that it's become more regular, and you have introduced other people too?

Yes, definitely. And I have tried to get my students to do it as well and I've found out how many colleagues walk for mental health reasons and for exercise reasons and they are only too happy to combine work and walk. So, yes, I believe that this process does work, it's not perfect but time and juggling work and family and everything else is probably always going to be an issue. The method helps enough to make that juggle more manageable.

But we are not saying that it must be walking, are we?

Oh no definitely not.

It could be any other activity that you agree on, the point is the commitment to a programme of activity. To discuss your creativity and agree to do something, so that there is a real commitment to a project and a framework. *Do you feel within that though, if your creative sense of self has shifted or changed at all, that it's linked to this process? Are there any new methods that you have started using or have changed during this time?*

I think the structure has been an important focus. Before this process started, I had stopped painting and I had left the studio and I am now painting pictures about the walks and now I have started to explore ideas that sit outside this walking process on my own, but that has only just started to happen so that's another shift. You have asked if my methods or process have changed, I think I have enacted something that I believe in which is setting up a method, a research project and we have been experimenting and are open to seeing what comes out of that process.

MA students often come to the course saying, "I want to finish this novel" or "I really want to do a script" and then after a few months this often changes, a project changes but the fact is that they have committed to a course, to working with like-minded people, hearing their ideas, exploring new ideas, and trying not to be too fixed about it as well. It's those people that seem to get most out of the course. Because there's not that disappointment of, "I didn't finish that book," or "I've realised that I am a poet, not a novelist" and that's okay, you know?

We are nearing the end of this project now and we trust that we will get to the end of this project now, so what next?

I hope that we can develop the work that we have already done with the Network of International Women Migrants, Asylum Seekers and Refugees or with other similar groups of women in a similar situation because that is very rewarding and really feels like we are building a creative community where it's needed. Because the workshops were really appreciated, and I think finding an audience for this work and this process seems to be important. And I think for me, also making sure I give time to my painting, that I manage to produce a body of work that I feel proud of, that I want to show, is important too.

And that is huge. I am so excited to see the exhibition that you are planning in the spring. I can't wait.

And you?

I have accepted that I don't see a role for myself in management where it would be creatively more stifling, and instead I want to focus on carving out more time for research and getting more time to do projects and writing. I also want to build on the art class I did and be open to taking more risks with my creativity, rather than telling people what they should be doing with their creativity, I want to allow myself to be open to people directing me.

I think what is important to me is that we really celebrate and hold onto this idea of looking back, of reflecting, thinking about things that have inspired and nourished us as well as things we have found difficult. Also, this time for walking, collaborating, being open to new ideas whilst also having a clear timetable and purpose is a method that we believe in and that's something we are ready to share with other people, isn't it? We need to celebrate that as part of the going forward.

Yes, and sharing is part of that. Sharing with other people and community groups might also be a way to test out the model and develop it. It's a bit like we have done the pilot run, now let's take it out and about.

Conclusion

The possibility of change

Jess

The optician tells me I need glasses and I feel lucky. Lockdown has taken its toll on my eyes, my confidence with hugging friends and my ability to stay awake and this is okay. Against the backdrop of Brexit, environmental catastrophe, the detrimental effects of a Tory government and a global mental health crisis, the ones I love emerge unscathed, keen to make new memories and welcome the changes the vaccine will eventually bring. Fading eyesight and a cure for insomnia are almost embarrassing side-effects but then, when I visit the GP for a check-up, she smiles kindly when she says I am peri-menopausal at 43. This is new.

Things are shifting, as they do. Sometimes when change comes it creates panic. We freeze in the headlights of the potential it brings. Motherhood, grief, cancer, work, patriarchy, politics have all induced moments of despair that impacted on my creativity, making me feel as if I was stuck or falling – like the woman in the picture Chris gave me all those years ago. The method we have devised in this book has made me feel more open to the possibility that getting stuck, falling, might be okay.

Life events that shape and shift us can and do result in an altered creativity. *The Year of Magical Thinking* by Joan Didion (2006) is a reflection on the time soon after her husband died. It is heart-breaking and life affirming, as is *To The River* by Olivia Laing where the author walks the River Ouse and bathes in nature to ease the pain of a breakup. In Katherine May's *Wintering* (2020) the writing is motivated by a time of necessary hibernation that inspires reflection; but whilst all these texts detail sorrow, loss, an identity crisis of some sort, they all result in work that is artistically profound, moving, expert, personal. Working with Chris, developing our method of walking, sharing, reflecting, and making has formed a pivotal part of the scaffold that has supported me through and over having cancer, feeling stifled, and Covid. We committed to each other and this way of working, and now a book that weaves our critical thinking and autobiographical words and arts has been sifted out of the legacy of debris that these events brought about. I look at chapter headings, pages, pictures and sections and think, this is it. A perfectly imperfect mirror of our experiences of this time. A way out of the freeze that our anxieties initiated. A move away from the headlights that our illnesses and stresses intensified and that we have now escaped.

As I walk out of the surgery, the peri-menopause diagnosis and thoughts of HRT and more change are stuck in my chest. An internal alarm threatens to go off inside my lungs.

Breathe.

Change will inevitably come. Grief, panic and worry cannot be dodged, and, when they hit, they often hit hard, throwing us up in the air, and where and how we fall, is uncertain but nearly always painful and discombobulating. This method with Chris has provided a first aid kit for my creativity and for me. Whether I fall or fly, I know my writing (and new artistic endeavours) can offer a vital part of my recovery. So let change – THE change even – come. I won't always be ready but, because of my work with Chris and the support our process has offered, I now feel less afraid, open to what might grow from the necessary mess.

Chris

> To be fully alive, the future is not ominous but a promise; it surrounds the present like a halo. It consists of possibilities that are felt as a possession of what is now and here. In life that is truly life everything overlaps and merges.
>
> (Dewey: 1934, p.15)

Things have changed, and not just in my creative life. After years of procrastinating, my husband, John, and I are moving out of the family house where we brought up our children and moving to something smaller, neater, less expensive. Accepting, I think, that the children are grown, my role has changed and whilst they visit, they don't live with us anymore. Until now, I was reluctant to accept this reality, a reality postponed when adult children temporarily descended to escape the challenges of Lockdown London, but evident again in the empty bedrooms, the reduced shopping bill and the free choice over evening TV programmes. But I am ready now. And family life is shape shifting too, because my beautiful daughter, Lizzie, and her partner, Abi, have had a truly adorable baby daughter, Eleanor, three weeks old at the time of writing. Gorgeous, gorgeous, gorgeous is what I want to say when I see her little face and when I think back to what my grandparents meant to me and the ways they shaped my life and my creativity, it will be a privilege and honour to pass on this love and support in whatever way she needs it.

Things have changed creatively too, aside from interruptions brought about by Covid restrictions. I am back at the studio, working once more amongst a community of fellow artists and I absorb so much simply by being in this shared and open space with people who are creative. Significantly, I no longer mourn abandoning oil paints and have enjoyed experimenting with new water-based media such as acrylics and watercolours. I have discovered that as well as allowing me to tread more lightly on the planet because they are less toxic, less polluting, better for health, the new media have allowed me to work in a different way – quicker and freer, and I remain open and curious about how these changes will present in my paintings and other artworks. When I pick up my brushes again, I find that alongside the more familiar figurative work, new abstract painting is emerging. This is new, unsettling, exciting and I am curious about what these shifts mean for the work that I will do in the future.

Figure 51: Infinite possibilities

Looking back at the imagery I have made during this journey, I reflect that I can see some of the effort I have made to control the controllable in my life, the neat, tentative line drawings I initially used to document my experience of the walks, and – although there is a part of me that would like to edit them out and include images that have more flourish, more polish – I leave them be because they mark a moment in my experience and are a record of all that has been. I leave them in peace, and they remain.

And I am delighted and surprised to find that I am an author, and this change feels important and significant in the sense that my creative sense of self has shifted and expanded to include writing. Alongside my painting practice, writing gave me space for personal reflection and a means of sharing these thoughts and feelings with Jess in a way that was nurturing and empowering because I could see my experience there on the page. Somehow, the writing – together with the walking and talking – helped me to let go piece by piece, bit by bit, of all the reasons I had become creatively stuck. And although writing about myself autobiographically has felt important and necessary to my creative recovery, I don't feel like I want to dwell there. I need to move on, look outwards towards others, embrace all the possibilities that the universe is sending my way.

I say a silent word of thanks to Jess for accompanying me on this journey, for I know that without this collaboration I would not have ventured so far, been as brave, or made as much progress with my recovery as I have. I feel that the strength of our collaboration was that each of us was uplifted by the other and we learnt to move as quickly or as slowly as the other could manage through the agreed creative tasks. This meant that sometimes one of us lagged behind or forged ahead, but we made progress as swiftly or slowly as our collective endeavours allowed. It was a forgiving and kind space, as well as a creative one. That, and the commitment to write, to make, to not let Jess down, pushed me past my resistance, my reluctance, my ability to succumb to the diversions that steered me away from what matters to me – an interwoven mix still of health, family and friends and my creative practice. I reflect that illness, like any life crisis, is all-consuming for a time and sometimes it's hard to focus on what else matters to you, but the space that we created of mutual support and encouragement provided a way for us to first remind ourselves and tease out what important to us, what we wanted to spend our time doing right now – but also our hopes for the future – and ensure that we progressed these things in tangible ways. Thus, with every conversation, every piece of writing, with every piece of art made, we created the possibility of a new revived creativity.

End of the book

Illness brought change: a change that impacted on our understanding of ourselves and our perspective on the world. We both felt our creativity had withered, that illness had hampered us and our practices of art and writing. But we have found that the model we developed revitalised our creativity in a way that has been exciting, surprising, and profound. We believe that the method of walking/doing, discussing/reflecting and making, can and did inspire, re-engage and reshape our creativity. This practice, unsure and tentative at first, has moved us through our experiences with cancer and creative blocks and helped us produce new work. The book that you are reading is the growth our process has germinated.

Our model offers a supportive framework with stepping-stones towards a creative recovery. It is, first and foremost, a process that helps you to make space for your creativity as you commit to the programme that the book suggests. The programme offers a sense of direction and opens your awareness to the possibility that things can be different, perhaps even better, in the future. It acknowledges uncertainty and offers no guarantees, but we have argued that our creativity is richer because we committed to this programme, and we are different because of it. There is a renewed sense of going forward, of direction and possibility.

Drawing on personal histories, autobiographical experiences and exploring them directly and indirectly in our work helped to unlock and draw out our creativity after a fallow period. Our creativity comes from us, and by using our lives as a source of inspiration we are validating who we are, where we have been and what has happened to us. This method can inspire and support our creativity and a creative recovery. Memories and narratives of our lives provide starting points for exploring creative ideas, and we have found that the work that we do, the writing and the artwork, is more powerful and potent because it comes from this deep and personal place of knowing, from our histories. We urge you to make work that comes from you and is connected to you and remember that your autobiographical memories and experiences provide a storehouse of ideas that you can draw on to support your creativity at any time.

Our creativity has been transformed by the collaborative process at the heart of this method because the artworks we make and the writing we do arise from dialogue and shared reflections. They support us to move on from a world and view of creativity where we are solely focused on our individual concerns to a world where we share our thoughts and creativity with others, allowing us to extend and build a creative community to support ourselves and each other. And sharing this process and these artworks with others and encouraging people to reflect on their experiences, to see their contributions as unique, is important. It provides a space for these stories to be seen, heard and valued.

We believe that it is the dialogue, shared reflection, and our commitment to extending our community via you, the readers, the people we work with and the future work we will make as a result of this new method that makes our work distinct. The communal aspect has fortified and sustained us, helped us to come to know each other, our creativity and ourselves differently. It has helped us to respect and value the women we are in a way that seemed unthinkable when we began the process. We both felt depleted and changed but now we feel changed and restored. To restore something is to bring something back, return it to a former glory but of course part of this process involves changing it, using new materials or methods to bring something back. This isn't always positive: in 2010 the Italian prime minister Silvio Berlusconi insisted that the missing body parts of Venus and Mars (circa 175 CE) be restored, saying that they were incomplete (Willey, 2010). The added hand and penis outraged many critics and eventually, the appendages were removed again. We do not seek to deny or paint over our experiences, rather we now feel able to progress our creative, personal and professional lives, accepting that we are women who have had cancer, we are women whose creativity sometimes falters, and we are still more than enough.

In her book, Margaret Wheatley identifies conversations as being the simplest way to restore hope, suggesting that by sharing our stories, problems will lessen, and we will feel more able to cope with an uncertain future (Wheatley, 2002). As we all emerge from the enforced hibernation that the pandemic brought, political, environmental and personal landscapes are altered. There is a new terrain that needs to be navigated, mapped and traversed. Writing and making cannot halt climate change or Brexit or eradicate grief, but they can and must capture and reflect and reimagine this time. Paulo Freire suggests that in order to escape or change bleak situations, humanity requires a politics of hope and to love and trust fellow humans, no matter how broken the world seems. It stems from 'an ontological need' (Freire: 1994, p.10) and we have learnt that dialogue and creativity can not only ease us back into life post-Covid, but also offer us a way to process and reconnect after what has come to pass. Sharing (real and imagined) stories of this time – and voicing our fantasies and goals for what is to come – will allow us to move forward instead of feeling frozen, unable to move or think or dream further than this time. Co-production has always had an important role to play in rethinking and remaking the world for the better (Daykin et al: 2017) and our way of working relies on collaboration, on valuing others, and on hope.

We have come to understand the importance of walking as an embodied approach to our creative recoveries and this was crucial because our illness and trauma involved our bodies and we instinctively felt that walking could be central to our recoveries. We simply knew that we could not be passive; we needed to move, surround ourselves with nature and empower our bodies in a way that felt supportive – encouraging us to heal, to live, to experience the world again and create new memories and experiences, step by step, walk by walk, that would distance us from illness and feeling creatively moribund.

Each walk meant there was time and space during which we could acknowledge and express ourselves and talk about what mattered to us in that moment: talking whilst we were walking and reflecting on the conversation by writing these events afterwards. And the time of the walk – away from the distractions of work, family, social media – meant there was time to really listen to and reflect on what the other person was saying and to be heard in a way that was supportive and encouraging.

In this way we felt supported to acknowledge the reality of our lives, the lack of certainty for the future, but interspersed with these sometimes difficult conversations there were increasingly fragments of our plans to progress our project and so glimmers of hopes for the future. And because we were walking and talking away from the office, away from the studio, we found there was time to be heard in a way that was sustaining, rare and important. These conversations were not always easy to listen to or to participate in. They were sometimes uncomfortable and sometimes upsetting and painful, but they were also uplifting, encouraging, joyful and welcomed, because through these events we were figuring out and attending to what mattered to us.

In this shared space of walking and dialogue we were able to acknowledge the reality of our situation, the lack of certainty about the future but also not to dwell there as we begin to interweave and seed ideas for our creative future so helping to bring hope and light into our lives. Could we have achieved as much individually? Perhaps, but it is not a thought we choose to dwell on. For us, identifying a friend you trust and who you can work through your own recovery with, is intrinsic to this process. It is collaborative, connected, shared. We are now seeking to extend this connection to other people who feel creatively stuck – via this book but also through future projects where we will interview people about their creativity and identify other tools to help us map a way over, under and through these times.

Task

Taking Stock and Moving Forward

Think back to when you started the book and think about the following:

- What are you writing/drawing/painting/filming/performing/making now?

- How has your creativity changed and how has it remained the same?
- Do you feel differently about your creativity and your creative self?
- Do you know what you will do next to support and value your creativity?

We encourage you to embark on a shared creative endeavour using the method of:

- Getting away from conventional work/personal spaces, moving – we chose walking.
- Dialogue – purposeful conversation about work, creative process, health.
- Writing/making – about the experience of the walk itself and any stories/memories the process triggered.
- Feedback – reading each other's work and providing constructive critique including asking questions about what the work might mean.
- Reflection – how has the process made you both feel and what has it helped you to think/write/draw/paint/make about and why? What has changed and what has stayed the same – emotionally, professionally and in relation to creative process and practice?

Be open to what happens to your creativity and know that you will find the process to be challenging but also stimulating and supportive. By committing to an agreed project with a timeline, with a set of tasks and agreed goals for the project and by opening and engaging in a dialogue with another person about your experiences, your artwork, your writing challenges, you move away from your stuck place and embark on a process that creates movement and brings changes to your creativity. We hope that through the process you will broaden your vision and renew your focus and sense of creative purpose, that you will have a revived confidence in your creative self.

The support of another person is crucial as they bear witness to your transformation and can support you through moments of difficulty or doubt. Perhaps more importantly, this connection will encourage you to be interested in the life and creativity of another human being as well as your own and bring you to an understanding that your creativity is interwoven with the world outside your own experience whilst also acknowledging that it is a deep and important part of who you are. It needs celebrating, documenting, and legitimising. You are here. You matter. You make.

List of Figures

Bibliography

Daykin, N., Gray, K., McCree, M. & Willis, J. (2017) 'Creative and credible evaluation for arts, health and well-being: opportunities and challenges of co-production', *Arts & Health*, 9:2, 123-138

Didion, J. (2006) *The Year of Magical Thinking*, Harper Perennial

Freire, P. (1994) *Pedagogy of Hope*, Continuum

Laing, O. (2019) *To the River*, Canongate

May, K. (2020) *Wintering*, Rider

Wheatley, M., (2002) 'Turning to one another: Simple conversations to restore hope to the future', *The Journal for Quality and Participation* 25.2: 8

Willey, D. (2010) 'Italian PM 'enhances' ancient Roman statues', *BBC News,* 18 November 2010. https://bit.ly/creativeAE

Creative Recovery

We meet in car parks,
Spaces people pass through
At times where day and night tussle
In the half-light of dawn or dusk.
We are neither here nor there,
Unsure exactly where we should be,
Traversing the liminal and the luminal
On our way to a place
We can't yet name.

Watched by sparrows and seagulls,
We speak instead of where we have been.
Your grandmother with her barrow,
St Martin's and the Tate,
Your father always shape-shifting yet
Somehow the same.
The ring I didn't want or need
And the wedding cancer made you miss.
Parsnip soup I turned down in your kitchen,
The woman flying or falling – we still aren't sure.
2 hard-fought PhDs, 2 easier chapters,
Articles written in-between feeds and trying to breathe.
You still won't say you are a writer,
A hat you can't wear lightly,
But reaching back now, *we both know.*

Climbing stiles and making our own way,
Steps becoming surer in thickest mud,
We speak of stuck places and slip ups,
With our eyes on the horizon
Refusing to turn or double back.
You have captured us in tinctures
Of rose and fern and tan.
Where we are magical and moving,
Known and still unknown,
Framed on a canvas but travelling still.
Only covid, cows and cancer make us doubt the way

But we walked through them before
We know the sounds and terrain.

We complete big loops that bring us back.
We walk aligned but not the same.
We sense each other's hurt and see the gold in our scars,
You won't call yourself a writer,
The word cancer still gets stuck
In my throat.
We chart a future of our design,
We imagine where it leads and what we can hope for,
We fold this map into edges and corners,
Push it out into the world to catch an airstream and alight.
We will watch it glide and fall and rise again.
And try not to mind
That we won't ever know
Quite where it stops

Where we land.

About the Authors

Dr Christina Reading is an independent artist and researcher who works on a variety of interdisciplinary and collaborative creative research projects with undergraduates, postgraduates and the wider community. Her work is united by an interest in, and commitment to, developing her and other people's creative learning and practice. She lives and works in Brighton with her family and continues to walk, make and write whenever she can.

Dr Jess Moriarty is Principal Lecturer in Creative Writing at the University of Brighton where she is co-director for the Centre of Arts and Wellbeing. She has published on autoethnography, Creative Writing pedagogy and community engagement. Jess lives in Brighton with her family and continues to walk every day.
https://research.brighton.ac.uk/en/persons/jessica-moriarty

Also from Triarchy Press

Walking Bodies ~ edited by: Helen Billinghurst, Claire Hind & Phil Smith
A curated collection of papers, provocations and actions from the 'Walking's New Movements' conference held at the University of Plymouth in November 2019.

walk write (repeat) ~ Sonia Overall
Offering a whole array of sparks, experiments, projects, catapults, prompts, drifts and exercises, this is a manual for creative writers. Use it to generate ideas, create text and read differently.

On Walking... and Stalking Sebald ~ Phil Smith
Sets out a kind of walking for which the author has become very well known. It's a kind of walking that burrows beneath the guidebook, looks beyond the Tudor facade and feels beneath the blisters. Those who try it report that their walking is never the same again.

Walking Art Practice ~ Ernesto Pujol
Combining elements from an art book, field journal and walkers' manifesto, this is a text for performative artists, art students, and all who walk as cultural activism. It brings together the author's experiences as a monk, performance artist, social choreographer and educator. They serve as a provocation, walkers' manifesto and teaching guide.

Guidebook for an Armchair Pilgrimage ~ Phil Smith, Tony Whitehead & John Schott
"It is wonderful – a brilliant idea, beautifully done, with a sweetly companionable tone to the writing." Jay Griffiths (writer/broadcaster/author)

Nature Connection ~ Margaret Kerr & Jana Lemke
A compact handbook of nature practices for personal development and coaches, therapists and outdoor educators.

www.triarchypress.net/walking